★★★

Real Estate

★★★

William H. Pivar
Richard W. Post

Real Estate
Education Company
a division of Dearborn Financial Publishing, Inc.

While a great deal of care has been taken to provide accurate and current information, the ideas, suggestions, general principles and conclusions presented in this text are subject to local, state and federal laws and regulations, court cases and any revisions of same. The reader thus is urged to consult legal counsel regarding any points of law—this publication should not be used as a substitute for competent legal advice.

Executive Editor: Kathleen A. Welton
Acquisitions Editor: Wendy Lochner
Copy Editor: Lois Smit
Interior Design: Sara Shelton
Cover Design: Mary Kushmir

Published by Real Estate Education Company,
a division of Dearborn Financial Publishing, Inc.

91 10 9 8 7 6 5 4 3 2

Library of Congress Cataloging-in-Publication Data

Pivar, William H.
    Power real estate negotiation/William H. Pivar, Richard W. Post.
      p. cm.
    Includes index.
    ISBN 0-88462-898-1
  1. Real estate business. 2. Negotiation in business. I. Post,
Richard W. II. Title.
HD1379.055 1989   89-12591
333.33'068—dc20   CIP

Contents

Introduction

Negotiation is a skill, and, like any skill, the rudiments can be learned. Almost anyone can become a creditable negotiator, and with practice and preparation can become an outstanding negotiator.

Negotiation really is a process, a process of reaching an agreement. It involves a mutual movement of positions until a meeting of the minds can be obtained. If such an agreement is not reached, the process has failed. Anything short of an agreement in negotiation is really failure. An agreement is a solution to a problem which both sides are willing and able to accept. It will be somewhere between the seller's initial position, usually an asking price, and the buyer's initial offering price.

While it is generally in the best interests of negotiating parties to reach agreement, each side strives to maintain its initial position with as few and as minor changes as possible.

Most major purchases, from large industrial contracts to the more common purchase of real estate, are the result of negotiations. Except for some new construction, negotiation is the general means of setting sale values and terms in real estate transactions. Even some builders who appear to have one-price policies will negotiate nonbasic price items such as lender costs and upgraded extras.

Don't regard negotiation with a negative viewpoint as haggling. Negotiation is the basis of our marketplace, where buyers and sellers arrive at values. Negotiation is not conflict; it is the resolution of conflict to meet the needs of the parties.

Negotiation is a problem-solving process. It is also an entirely voluntary process. The results are only what was agreed upon by the parties. You can get no more than the other party is willing to give, and you will give no more than you are willing to give.

Negotiation is also a discovery process, where you will both learn and inform. This discovery process generally results in parties making adjustments to their positions. As your negotiation skills develop, the greater will be the level of your achievements in negotiation. You will find that these skills will apply to all of your interpersonal relationships where conflicts arise. Many of the techniques of real estate sales and lease negotiation can solve conflicts inherent in our lives. Wherever a resolution of conflict is sought, the negotiation process is involved.

Negotiation can be a mutually satisfactory process, where both sides benefit. This is the best negotiation, a win-win negotiation. Agreements of this type are likely to be honored by the parties and often result in further beneficial agreements.

There are, however, some competitive people who want much more than just to win. They are not happy unless the other side clearly loses. They want a win-lose negotiation with themselves on the win side. These people are not well liked but seem to relish the reputation they develop. However, they usually make very few agreements. We hope you will learn from this book that you will be further ahead with a win-win attitude. "Neither a Scrooge nor a patsy be."

Included in this book are techniques we have used during years of negotiations, techniques others have used against us, as well as ideas from many other attorneys and negotiators. We are arming you with an arsenal of ideas to help you maximize your negotiation results.

1. Negotiation Planning

Planning involves setting goals, positions to be taken, techniques to be utilized and the preparation of facts and materials to support your position. It also involves an understanding of yourself, your adversary and the risk involved.

Qualities of a Good Negotiator

To be a good negotiator, you should be a good *researcher* (willing and able to find the facts prior to and during negotiations) and a good *listener* (able to listen to what the other party is really saying, not what you think he/she should be saying). In addition you should possess the following:

Patience—The ability to take your time in developing a position and communicating it to your adversary.

Persuasiveness—The ability to present your views in a convincing manner that sells benefits and overcomes objections.

Inventiveness—The ability to tailor solutions to the problem.

Flexibility—The ability to adapt your position as changes are indicated. (Having alternatives can avoid a hardened position that precludes a later agreement.)

Courage—The ability to maintain a position under fire.

Endurance—Staying power to maintain your position.

Inscrutability—Ability to conceal the extent of your desires and weaknesses.

Aggression—The ability to use your power when needed (really controlled aggression).

Should You Get Help?

People who avoid conflict make poor negotiators. They don't like to say no. If you have difficulty being obstinate or unreasonable, you might make a poor negotiator.

Some people get very agitated when faced with any unknown situation. These people should avoid negotiations.

People who lack self-assurance should avoid negotiation.

If you want to be loved, don't enter negotiations, as you are likely to give away the farm.

If one party is self-assured and the opponent has doubts and fears, the self-assured party is likely to end up dominating that opponent.

Some people worry about failure and how a spouse or other person will react to their losing.

All of these people should consider being an observer and letting a professional take over for them. They should consider hiring either a competent real estate broker or a real estate attorney to handle face-to-face negotiations. Attorneys are well prepared for such adversarial roles. Having your own negotiator makes sense. Chances are you will be able to engage an attorney for two half-days for $1,000, which could well save you many thousands of dollars in your final position. There are also any number of very competent real estate brokers who are willing to negotiate for a fee.

Win-Win

Most successful negotiations are really win-win situations, where both parties derive benefits from the agreement. Win-win negotiations are likely to be completed; but win-lose negotiations very often fail to close, even though an agreement was reached. When win-lose contracts are entered into, performance can become a problem. This is especially true of construction contracts. Often, the net result is a lose-lose situation, with both parties being hurt.

If you believe that negotiation must be a win-lose situation (with a winner and loser), chances are you will complete very few deals and will waste a great deal of your time in unsuccessful negotiations.

Negotiations become an ego trip with some persons. They not only want to win, they want the other side to lose. Some negotiators actually want to humiliate their opposition. These persons have to win. They take an ironclad position and refuse to budge. When they're dealing from a position of sufficient strength, they do win—but not very often. More likely, they just waste a great deal of time.

Don't be taken in by first impressions. Just because the other party smiles a lot doesn't mean he or she has good intentions. The cat smiles at the canary.

Beware the opponent who says both parties must benefit in any negotiations, the person who tells you negotiation to be successful must be a win-win situation. Everyone with this initial approach isn't after everything you have. However, when you're negotiating with an adversary who won't settle for anything less than unconditional surrender, and your humiliation as well, you can expect him or her to start with espousing the mutual benefits of negotiation.

In the stock market there is a saying: "The bulls can make money, the bears can make money, but the pigs always lose." This applies to negotiations as well. If you are a pig and get too greedy, the result is going to be no deal.

In a period of real estate inflation, looking for that big bargain can be a bad way to go. As an example, during much of 1988 the values of residential property in Huntington Beach, California, rose 5 percent per month. Therefore, waiting 6 months to be able to buy a property 10 percent below what you regard as market value could mean a loss of at least 20 percent.

Risks of Negotiations

While risks must be taken if you are to negotiate, you must nevertheless understand the risks and the alternatives to them before you take those risks.

As a buyer trying to negotiate the price down, or as a seller trying to negotiate an offer up, you are taking a risk. You are risking, as a buyer, that another buyer might offer the asking price or that the seller might decide to take the property off the market. As a seller, you risk the danger that the buyer will find another property that better meets his or her needs or will change his or her mind about purchasing.

Your willingness to accept risk of no sale or purchase and the degree of risk you will accept influences your negotiation plan. If you as a seller are unable to take any risk, accept the offer made because with a counteroffer you release the offeror. As a buyer, you should realize that some deductions can be made from a seller's position with very little risk. As you increase your demands, risks do occur. Besides the risk of another buyer or seller or the decision not to sell, there is also the risk the other party will become so alienated, because of your position, that meaningful communication is impossible.

When Not To Negotiate

Don't negotiate if it is not necessary. If you're in a position of such power, where concessions on your part will not be necessary to make a contract, you can be a one-price seller with stated terms.

Face to Face

The more knowledgeable you are as a buyer, the greater the benefits of face-to-face negotiations. The advantages of such negotiations are:

1. Many people find it harder to reject a face-to-face offer than a written one.
2. Written negotiations don't allow a discovery process.
3. You cannot get a feel for a person's needs unless you deal directly.
4. Face-to-face encounters allow you to work out areas of contention quickly.
5. In complex situations, written negotiations are impractical because of the number of issues and possible alternatives involved.

If you have been shown property by an agent, you must consider the agent in the negotiations. Most real estate negotiations are done through agents; buyer and seller seldom meet. Agents have an ungodly fear of buyers getting together with sellers because the seller might say something that will ruin the deal.

If you feel competent, or have an agent or attorney who will negotiate for you, then arrange for a face-to-face meeting. Inform the agent you're interested in discussing a purchase with the owner and ask the agent to set up the meeting. Do not discuss the offer with the agent. Because the agent has a duty to present every offer, you really have the power to insist on the face-to-face meeting. Keep in mind that contractually the agent will probably be representing the seller, not you. You don't want to antagonize the agent, but you do want a meeting. A statement such as "I think you're going to earn a commission today" can be very helpful.

Phone Negotiations

If you negotiate by phone, have a written plan and an outline of points to be covered. Confirm any agreement immediately in writing, as memories tend to fade or undergo adjustment with time

Know the Property

Because a property appeals to a buyer, the buyer may wish to rush into negotiations to secure the property before anyone else gets it. Avoid the rush; it takes only a few hours to learn a great deal about a property. You could discover major problems, and, if there are none, you will have gained peace of mind.

You can hire a structural inspector who will survey the property for you. This type of inspection may reveal latent as well as patent defects. A simpler and quicker method might be to talk to a few neighbors, tenants and property supervisors. Let them know you're interested in purchasing the property. You will generally find neighbors eager to tell you good and bad points about a property and the neighborhood. You can also discover information about owners and tenants. Asking the building supervisor if he or she would be willing to stay if you purchase the building will provide excellent information. If the property has professional management, ask if it would be willing to continue managing the property if you purchase. You will find the company's attitude suddenly becomes quite cordial.

Talk to as many people as you can who are familiar with the property, as one may know something another does not. Information about tenants can also be important. In one case a prospective buyer discovered the tenant with a long-term lease on a special-purpose structure had just declared Chapter 11 bankruptcy.

Value

Don't negotiate in a vacuum. Establish value before you sit down to negotiate. By checking list prices of similar property you don't establish value, only what others are setting as an initial position. Sale prices, however, can be used to establish value.

Whether you are a buyer or a seller, knowing recent comparable sales or lease prices can prepare you to influence the other party. It is hard to argue with facts. If you have an agent or are an agent, the local multiple-listing services as well as large property management firms can provide you with this information. If you do not have an agent, many brokers and/or appraisers will put together a comparable package for a fee.

If you are unsure of value, it would be worth your while, either as a buyer or seller, to pay for a professional appraisal. Generally, the designation MAI (Member of the Appraisal Institute, American Institute of Real Estate Appraisers) or SREA (Society of Real Estate Appraisers) indicate a high level of competence. You can also use the appraisal findings as a tool in negotiation if you are willing to buy (or sell) at the appraised evaluation. Just because you get a seller to accept significantly less than had been asked or a buyer to raise the offer significantly does not mean you made a reasonable deal. Keep in mind that paying more does not increase the worth of what you are buying, nor does accepting less decrease its worth.

Gross Rent Multiplier

The gross rent multiplier indicates how many times its gross income a property is selling for. It can be expressed as a monthly or annual figure. To determine the gross multiplier, divide the selling price by the gross income. If similar properties are selling for nine times gross income, a property selling at $7^{1}/_{2}$ times gross would seem to be a bargain; however, this is not necessarily so. Gross figures do not indicate unusual expenses or risks associated with a particular property. Gross is not net. While some investors use the gross multiplier to determine values, don't do it. Like most things that are easy, it isn't really worthwhile. Using the gross rent multiplier as the basis of your negotiating position is an invitation to financial disaster.

Your Adversary

Know as much as possible about your adversary. If your adversary has had dealings with others, check with these parties prior to your negotiations. Of special interest to you is the person's integrity. If he or she has balked at performance after agreement, tried to find faults to further negotiate after negotiations were completed, or has been litigious in the past, consider if you really want to negotiate with that person. You want to buy an agreement, not a lawsuit.

Besides reasons for buying or selling, litigious nature of your adversary and his or her integrity, other specific questions of interest to you include the following.

Questions about Sellers

How long has the property been on the market?
Were there any prior offers? If so what were they?
If any prior offer was accepted, why did the sale not close?
What did seller pay?
What was the cost of any improvements made by seller?
What are the terms of all leases?
What is the financial strength of the seller?
What is the financial strength of the tenants?
What is the likelihood of tenants remaining?
What is the difference, if any, between contract rent (lease) and economic rent (what property is actually worth)?
What is the current financing (if assumable)?
What are the costs and terms of any new financing?
What is the likelihood of seller financing?

Questions about Buyers

Who are buyers?
Are they investors or users?
What is their financial strength?
What else have they purchased? Where? For how much?

Motivations and Needs

If you understand your adversary, you can formulate a position that can benefit him or her and best meet your needs as well. Put yourself in the other party's shoes as to motivation and needs.

What do you suppose would be the minimum this person would accept for the property or the maximum he or she will pay? (Remember these figures are prenegotiation. Hopefully, by negotiating you will be able to lower expectations of sellers and raise the willingness of buyers.)

A danger in negotiation preparation is to evaluate your opponent's likely position by your own experiences. Instead, try to place yourself in your opponent's place and base your estimate on your opponent's background and aspirations. When you underestimate your opponent's power, you may walk away from negotiations without an agreement. If you overestimate your opponent's power, you will probably get an agreement in which you will pay more or get less than would otherwise be possible. You really want the reverse to happen. You want your adversary to overestimate your power. If you get everything you desired in negotiations, chances are your aspiration level was too low.

Litigious People

There are some buyers and sellers who seem to love litigation. They use the courts as a final negotiation technique to get one more bite out of the apple which could be you. One gentleman in California has achieved national fame for his lawsuits. He has sued, usually successfully, neighbors, relatives, people he has done business with and even government officials. He is given a wide berth by people who know of his inclination to use the courts.

When you deal with litigious buyers or sellers you risk purchasing a costly lawsuit. Check with people who have done business with the other party. Check the county courthouse plaintiff and defendant indexes. A person who has often been a plaintiff is likely to be of a litigious nature, and you may want to check with several of the defendants in such cases. On the other hand, a person who is a defendant in a number of lawsuits might be the type who does not live up to his or her agreements or who has been guilty of questionable conduct. Check with several plaintiffs in these cases.

In New York, many landlords won't lease to attorneys, as too often disagreements end up in court. Several large national brokerage firms report particularly high percentages of sales to lawyers (or instances where they represented lawyers) that ended in lawsuits.

Life is too short for you to buy unnecessary trouble. While Will Rogers said he never met a person he didn't like, he probably didn't do business with many of them.

Seller's Motivation

The key to your position as buyer, and to whether you want to bother to negotiate, is the seller's motivation. If a seller doesn't need to sell, and will only sell if the price is high enough, the chance of getting the property at a fair price is not very good. This type of seller usually overprices the property to start with and is unlikely to make significant concessions.

Must-sell sellers—those who are motivated—are the people you really want to negotiate with. Examples of this type of motivation are divorce, death, partnership dissolution, etc. Out-of-the-area sellers are generally more motivated to sell than local owners. Owners of property with vacancies or tenant problems are more motivated than owners of property with few problems. Financial difficulties of all types make for motivated sellers.

At times, owners will announce their motivations in ads. "Divorce forces sale of . . . ." Real estate agents will generally not reveal the reason for selling unless the seller authorizes it because strong seller motivation puts the buyer in a power situation. The more desperate the seller, the more power you have as buyer.

Often, the best approach is straightforward: "Why are you selling?" If the reason indicates a high motivation to sell, the owner has put you in a power position. If the reason given does not indicate a strong need to sell, it may or may not be accurate.

Checking with tenants and/or neighbors might well reveal reasons not given by the owner.

Lease Motivation

If you know the owner has a negative cash flow on a structure that has a great deal of vacant space, you as a prospective tenant are in a power situation. The more space you are interested in, the more powerful your position becomes.

Often, such property is also for sale. If so, it is an indication that the owner can't or doesn't want to continue with the negative cash flow, making your position as a prospective lessee even more powerful. Ask about operating expenses, present income and debt service. You will then know the owner's cash short fall each month, which further enhances your power. For example, a lease proposal that just allows the owner to break even on cash flow would have an excellent chance of being accepted if the property had been vacant for a long period and there is a high area vacancy rate.

Check the Neighbors

When you are negotiating the sale of raw land, contact neighboring property owners. If the buyers have concluded the purchase or option on neighboring property, they are probably assembling a large parcel for a particular purpose. This would change the ground rules. Your expectations should immediately expand, as you now have far more power than you imagined. Even if neighboring owners have not been approached to sell their property, you want to know if they will consider selling. If you can get a short-term option to buy for a nominal sum, with the right to extend the option upon the payment of a greater sum of money, then for a few dollars you might have an excellent bargaining chip. You temporarily control the neighboring property and can transfer that control. Even to a buyer who really doesn't need it now, the control is tantalizing.

Be careful. You don't want to offer options at less than you want for your property, as you will be giving your buyer strong ammunition for a lower sales price.

Sellers Who Haven't Given Listings

While at times you can make exceptional purchases directly from sellers, most motivated sellers give listings to agents because they realize most sales are made through agents. Many sellers who don't use agents are will-sell sellers; they don't have to sell, but will if the price is right. With such sellers it is unlikely you will be able to buy at market value, and don't even think of a below-market-value purchase.

Another problem in dealing with a seller not represented by an agent is that you can waste a great deal of time. Some sellers are testing the market more than trying to sell. When you think you are close to an agreement, this type of seller will withdraw the property from the market because all he really wanted was an idea of value.

If you're uncertain that a seller really will sell, you can save a great deal of time by simply asking for copies of all leases, tax statements and detailed operating statements. If the seller balks, chances are you have a seller who really isn't.

Buyer's Motivation

While it has often been said, "Love people, use things," many people have turned this around. A strong emotional attachment, where the buyer "just has to have it," is not unusual, especially for residential property. The stronger the buyer's emotional involvement, the greater the seller's power.

A buyer's purchase of other property in the area indicates assemblage for development or redevelopment purposes. This can give you extreme power in any negotiation.

When you have a special-purpose property and there are no similar properties currently available, what otherwise would be a white elephant puts you in a power position with a buyer who needs that particular type of property.

A buyer obviously in love with a property will cause an opponent to toughen up on what otherwise might have been a flexible position. If you are emotionally involved and feel you must have the property, don't wear your position on your sleeve. You want a mildly interested message to come through. If you can do this, your chance of a favorable end result will be significantly enhanced.

What They Paid

What a person paid for property does not affect the real value of the property, but it can affect the purchase price. When a seller is making a profit, a price reduction is far more likely than when the reduction results in a loss. Also, sellers are more likely to provide seller financing when they are financing profit dollars and ·not their original investment dollars.

The easiest way to find out what an owner paid for residential property is to ask neighbors. Chances are, one will know or be able to direct you to someone who does. By checking revenue or tax stamps on the previous seller's deed you can usually calculate sales prices. Employees of your county recorder's office can show you how to do this. Another way to discover sales price is to ask an owner during an informal conversation which agent he or she purchased the property through, and then contact that agent about similar properties. If you mention that [owner] had said he or she purchased through the agent and was quite happy, and then ask what was paid, you will usually get accurate data.

There are side benefits of this approach. You might obtain an informed estimate of present value and also develop a rapport with an agent who can lead you to other purchases.

Timing

Timing of a purchase should be considered in your planning. It affects your basic position. Time on market, previous offers and seller's motivation all affect your position. The longer a property has been on the market, the lower your offer and goal can be.

You may find a property has been on the market for two years with one previous offer that failed because of a buyer's inability to obtain financing. The seller is motivated to sell and ready for a low offer with no finance contingencies. With a property just coming on the market it is unlikely you would obtain a dramatic price reduction, although the seller would probably be more flexible on terms than on price.

Credit

You can waste a great deal of time with buyers/lessors who can't really buy or lease. Before serious negotiations, ask prospective buyers or lessors for a copy of their computer credit print out. They can request it from a local credit agency. (For firms, you can also check the Dun & Bradstreet rating.) Don't be awed by dress and manner. Remember, most con men dress like millionaires. Just because a person acts as if money is no problem doesn't mean he has any.

If a buyer balks at giving you credit data, the chances are he or she has problems. Most legitimate buyers or lessors are willing to have you verify their qualifications.

Just as you must qualify a buyer as to ability to provide cash and/or credit, you want to qualify a seller. Will the seller be able to deliver title? A property profile (often provided without cost) from a title insurance firm will tell you about liens against the property. If the seller isn't going to realize enough at sale to clear the liens, the chances of a sale completion are slim unless the creditors will agree to a compromise.

A side effect of a preliminary title report is that you could discover secret motivation of the seller, such as judgment creditors, which increases your power.

Predictable People

It has often been said that people are creatures of habit. This holds true even in negotiations. By checking with people who have previously done business with a seller, you might find a buyer customarily has started with a very low offer, which at times he or she has increased from 10 percent to 30 percent. Likely, that party's initial offer to you is around 30 percent less than he is willing to pay, but of course he will try to negotiate as low a purchase price as possible. Holding firm for a higher price and eventually coming down to the 30 percent increase range of predictability might be the way to maximize the price with that particular buyer.

Unknown Adversary

Before face-to-face negotiations, you want to know if the person you will be negotiating with has the final authority to approve the agreement. If he or she has partners, be certain the partners are there. You don't want to agree to a price and then have the partner say no and use your negotiated price as a starting point for a further assault on your pocketbook.

Never negotiate with people who want you to give concessions but really lack the authority to give concessions themselves.

Plan

As previously stated, you should consider your opponent's likely opening position and what he or she will or will not want to pay or accept. Your plan should be not only to change your opponent's aspiration level but to get him to reevaluate the minimum he will accept or the maximum he will pay.

Your overall plan should include how you visualize the negotiation process moving toward your desired conclusion. To achieve this, you must consider the basis of your opponent's position and the arguments your opponent will use. You must plan not only support for your position but arguments to weaken the position of your opponent. You should identify the obstacles you anticipate in negotiations and plan how to overcome them. (Specific arguments and tactics are covered in Chapters 3-6.)

For a lease negotiation, consider your position on type of lease, terms, and even the clauses of the lease, based on how you envision the future national and local economy, future competition and changes in your needs.

If you know something is going to be asked, be prepared for it. For example, if you're going to ask a seller to finance part of the purchase price you should have a current credit bureau printout of your credit.

Decide on what benefits you want to offer the other side and what benefits you want to use as bargaining chips to hold and later give up in negotiations. Planning should include more than just arguments to be used; it should also include the actual language of the presentation.

Your planning really involves three steps:

1. Gain information. You want to know as much as possible about the property, similar properties, and the area.
2. Set goals. Set reasonable objectives based on your perception of strengths and needs. (Goals are not the opening position.)
3. Plan the strategies you will use, including timing.

In planning your negotiations, keep in mind that you must adjust to individual circumstances and reactions.

What are the other parties' motivations? Knowing these will help you in determining your position. What are the other person's alternatives to reaching agreement with you? If the alternatives are unacceptable, then your position is strengthened.

In considering solutions to likely problems, concentrate on those that meet needs. For example, a retired couple might find an annuity type of payment attractive. Work on probabilities rather than possibilities. Don't spend your time on solutions that have little likelihood of acceptance.

In planning you should:

1. Identify the mutual interests of the parties (for example, both lessor and lessee might desire a long-term lease).
2. Analyze your strengths and the strengths of the other party as well as weaknesses. (This is very important in set-

ting positions.) Remember that, when you are selling, you are in a power position because you alone control this property. As a buyer across the table from a seller, consider that you are the only buyer. Both are power positions, but only if you realize the power and convey this realization to your opponent.

3. Define the issues of likely contention.
4. Consider possible alternatives where impasse might occur. The larger the number of alternative solutions, the greater the chance you will be able to resolve conflict.

Normally, we negotiate with incomplete knowledge of our opponent. However, a good early-on technique before you give your position is to ask questions. If you listen to the answers, you can gain a great deal of insight into your opponent's needs.

Even if your opponent has all the power, he or she will seldom realize his or her entire strength. It is human nature to worry and give to you strengths you do not have.

Power is the ability to influence the other party to reevaluate and modify its position. After you have set your opening position, the first person who must be convinced as to the merit of that position is you. By repeating arguments to yourself as to why your position is overly generous to your opponent, you can psych yourself up to believing in your position. This belief will come through in your negotiations and will serve as a tool to gain concessions.

When do opponents hold firm and when do they give? These decisions are based on their perception of your position and strengths—their perception of your perception of your power and their own needs.

Power does not always win; the perception of power is every bit as important as actual power itself. Negotiation skills can provide that perception. Without skill, power would always prevail.

As a buyer, your negotiation errors will likely be erased in a rising marketplace, but a declining market will amplify them, making the need for negotiation planning of critical importance.

Prioritize

Before negotiations prioritize your wants, rank them according to the following categories: (1) must have, (2) want but can be flexible to alternatives, (3) want but could give up, (4) don't need or want (but other party doesn't know it). The don't-need-or-want group could be very important later as bargaining chips (see Chapter 3).

Recognize Values

In preparing for negotiations, you must consider the value of options and priorities and what items are likely to be negotiable. Often, an owner will be unwilling to leave a new $500 window air conditioner but nevertheless be receptive to a price reduction of $2,000. While your opponent's values may be askew, you want yours to be straight.

Prepare Your Presentation

Your presentation must show how you are meeting the needs of the other party. You must sell benefits. For example, a low cash offer could have the benefits of (1) quick escrow, (2) no contingencies, (3) no special conditions or required seller repairs, (4) no carryback seller financing.

You might be prepared to show, if the seller accepted a full price offer with owner financing, that the loan would sell at a discount on the secondary mortgage market. This would give you the true value of a full price offer with owner financing. A comparison between your offer and a full-price owner-financing offer might reveal that your offer is better, or only a few percentage points below it.

You can see that negotiation is really selling. What you are selling are the benefits of your position.

Area Data for Buyer

Most chambers of commerce have reports, brochures and studies that make any area seem to be the most desirable one possible. This material, which is generally available at no cost, should be put together for the buyer or lessee of land or investment property. Also include a map, with the property location marked, and information on major existing and planned uses that could influence your particular buyer or lessee.

Visuals

To give credence to a position, consider charts or graphs. Pictures of comparable properties can have a strong influence when accompanied with sale or lease information.

Facts

Be prepared. Verify the facts you will use and do not accept hearsay. If you support a position with fallacious data, all of your credibility, as well as any reputation you might enjoy, will be lost. Above all, be honest.

Too Much Data

A prenegotiation tactic used by some sellers upon request for data is to give literally reams of information, copies of 40-page leases for every tenant, covenants, conditions and restrictions, plot maps, tax statements, operating statements, etc. Too much data reduces the likelihood of noting what is significant. When you have a great deal of financial data, consider having an accountant provide a summary. Have leases and other legal documents reviewed by an attorney. You want to know if there are any hidden surprises.

What Is To Be Negotiated

Prior to negotiation, develop a checklist of what will have to be agreed upon. Such a list reduces the chance of a problem arising later over a matter not covered by negotiations. Points to be negotiated might include:

Price
Earnest money
Increases in earnest money
Period to closing
Abstract or title insurance (who pays)
Inspection of property and correction of defects
Warranty as to condition
Maintenance until closing
Apportionment of closing costs
Personal property to be included
What will be regarded as fixtures
Date of possession
Assumption of insurance
Costs of new loan
Assumption or subject to loan
Contingencies
Seller financing
   Interest rate
   Amortization
   Late payments
   Due-on-sale clause
   Balloon payments

In a lease, a great deal more must be negotiated. A commercial lease might take several days to finalize, even when rent is agreed upon, because every clause must be negotiated.

Role-Playing

Role-playing can hone your negotiation skills. In role-playing, you imagine all types of opponent responses and decide the best way for you to respond. You then practice your responses either to yourself or out loud. Practice not only the words but your delivery as well. If you have imagined a situation before it comes up, you will be prepared for it.

An excellent approach is to have a spouse or team member play the adversary and go through mock negotiations. It may sound juvenile but it works, and many of the best negotiators learned by just this sort of practice. In law schools, moot court is really just an exercise in role-playing.

Opening and Closing

Plan strong opening and closing statements. Present your strongest argument last. People tend to remember quite well what you said first and last, but their memory of what was in between tends to be fuzzy. In your closing, present both sides of the argument. It will enhance your credibility. State your conclusion. Don't leave anything implied.

Both the opening and closing, as well as arguments described in Chapters 3–6, can be preplanned. The best planning will allow you to appear extemporaneous, talking as one friend to another. Practice before a mirror. Be careful that your presentation doesn't come across as a lecture or as if you are talking down to the other party. If this is the effect, your chances of an agreement are very slim.

Aim High

If you aim at the moon, you are less likely to end up in the mud. Studies have shown that the higher the aspirations of negotiators, the greater their results.

There is a danger of quoting too high a selling, or too low a buying, price and turning your opponent off, so you never get to the table. There is an advantage in avoiding quoting figures until you are in a position to negotiate.

Optimism is fine, but don't take a completely unrealistic approach unless you're prepared for a quick retreat from it.

If you believe a seller's price is firm, then it is firm, and to buy you will have to meet it. In actuality, it is rare to see a seller's position immune to negotiation. Therefore, if you believe the firm price is merely a trial position, chances are your perseverance will show your belief was a reality.

You must have a minimum or maximum price that you're willing to live with. Success to a negotiator is a relative term. Whether or not you were successful depends upon your aspirations. If you hoped to get a lot for $100,000 and had a maximum position of $110,000, then in buying the property at $95,000 you were tremendously successful—despite the fact the other party hoped to sell it at $90,000 but had a minimum price of $75,000. In this case, both parties would regard themselves as winners; but if each knew the position of the other, they would each regard themselves as losers.

Keep in mind you have no power in negotiations if you believe you are powerless. If you go into negotiations prepared to meet the seller's asking price or to accept the buyer's offer, you generally will.

First Offer

Your first offer doesn't necessarily have to be "reasonable." You don't want to offer a seller more than his or her bottom-line minimum price. If you do, all further negotiations will involve giving up your own money. You want the initial position below seller's minimum or above buyer's maximum. The advantage of face-to-face negotiation is the parties are before you so you will get a reaction, not a walk-away rejection.

In setting offers, think of the psychological effect. While $79,900 might be the offer you want to make (as it is still in the $70's), for all practical purposes it is an offer of $80,000. Therefore, as buyer, you should offer $80,000. For $100 more you will have materially increased the chance of acceptance. Conversely, if you are a seller, offering to cut the price to $80,000 is nowhere near as effective as agreeing to accept $79,900. People are not rational when they deal with numbers, so these picky distinctions are really material.

Succeeding

You can always successfully complete a negotiation if you are willing to give in to the other parties' wishes completely. As you become tougher and take stronger positions, the percentage of negotiations that lead to contracts decreases.

What If You Are Unsuccessful

Before negotiations begin, consider what will happen if you are unsuccessful. If the result would be disastrous financially and/or emotionally, your bottom-line position should be adjusted.

Often people get so emotionally involved they can't exist without a property. We see this at auctions, where buyers often overpay. While you should try to avoid emotional attachment, it is far easier said than done. As a word of encouragement, no price is too much to pay for property that gives you pleasure, and any price is too much if the property fails to do so.

You should regard offers as casting out bait for a fish. Never cast out unless you really want the catch. Don't get caught in the bargain syndrome ("At that price, I have to buy [sell] it."). Unless you have a plan for using the property, don't buy. Unless you either need the proceeds or can find a better use for the proceeds than in the current property, don't sell. Don't make deals for the sake of making deals. Deals without benefits are bad deals.

Keep in mind the goal of negotiations is agreement. Any negotiation that fails to conclude in agreement has failed.

How badly you want a property will affect your position. If you must have it, you should not risk protracted negotiations unless you can get to the negotiation table immediately.

Just as you should analyze how much risk you can take, how much risk the other side can take should be considered. If they must have the deal, then you are in a position of power.

The Team Approach

If you are negotiating with other people on your side, be certain that they know your negotiation plan and their place on the team. Generally, you should decide on a team leader. Team members should be expected to (1) answer specific questions when asked by the team leader and (2) provide reinforcement to the team leader's approach. Team members should not change direction in negotiations or modify the stand of the team leader without prior consultation. Of course, there may be times when a team member will do so as a matter of planned strategy. Even a husband and wife buying a house constitutes a team. If one spouse hopes to bargain and the other spouse says, "This is the house we want—write it up," all bargaining strength is lost. Understanding of the team plan by all team members and their role in the plan is vital.

The team leader should have many of the attributes of a good poker player. He or she should have the will to hold, based on evaluation of the negotiation power of others, yet know when to concede. He or she must not reveal a position in order to obtain the greatest number of concessions. A person who avoids conflict in daily life, preferring to concede rather than face disapproval, would make a poor team leader.

A team brainstorming session can be very valuable prior to negotiation. Using a what-if technique, the team can develop some excellent approaches that can be used in negotiations. In multimillion-dollar negotiations, teams often go through mock negotiations to prepare for the real thing. Some even use video-cameras to critique their performance. One large firm engages in mock negotiations to audition negotiators.

If you are negotiating against a team, having your own team can give you psychological support.

There is danger in team negotiations if you end up taking positions that are really public postures to look good for your team, but that are unlikely to result in agreement.

Before you bring in a team, consider that the chance of concluding the negotiation with an agreement decreases with the number of people in the negotiations. The greatest chance of success occurs in one-on-one negotiations.

Your Power

Even when you as a buyer have a weak position because you need the property, you are not without power. A seller can't sell or lease without a buyer or a lessee.

Your power may be far more than you perceive. For example, the seller could be desperate to sell; the owner could be desperate to lease because of a negative cash flow. Never negotiate from a feeling of weakness, as that weakness will be perceived by your opponent and will become a reality. Set your positions as if you had strength, and you are likely to find that you do.

2. Physical Aspects of Negotiation

Having a home-field advantage is a plus in negotiations. When you control the location, taking control of the agenda and the breaks seems natural.

When you negotiate at your home or place of business, you have a feeling of security. You have, in fact, a psychological advantage that will likely give you greater courage but increase the timidity of your adversary. At your location, you can more likely call on reinforcements, if necessary, to join you in negotiations or to serve as a psychological crutch.

When you negotiate at your adversary's place of business or home, you give up this home-court advantage. However, one advantage to negotiating at your opponent's location is that you can now employ the tactic of walking out, which you cannot do when negotiating in your office.

When you know several meetings will be necessary, consider having an initial meeting at your adversary's location. Use this as an exploratory session. Your adversary will feel in control of the nonthreatening environment. Since you have had the first meeting at your adversary's location, it will seem only fair when you suggest the next meeting be held at your location. This will be the important session, where the home-field advantage becomes significant.

Neutral Ground

If you can't have the home-field advantage, consider taking it away from your opponent. Suggesting a neutral location will generally be met with agreement because parties know it is basically fair. Many banks, savings and loan companies and escrow firms have meeting rooms available at no cost. Hotel rooms and clubs can also be used.

A restaurant or coffee shop is an excellent place to negotiate rather straightforward matters, since it offers a familiar, nonthreatening environment. Because it is a public place, parties are more likely to remain calm. However, this environment does not lend itself to lengthy, involved negotiations.

A neutral location for more complex negotiations, such as a commercial lease or a sale, where many issues will have to be resolved, should offer a private meeting room as well as access to a copy machine and coffee.

If more than one person will be involved on one or both negotiating teams, separate areas to caucus and go over positions and offers are important to consider.

Neutral ground has the added advantage of limited interruptions, as you are less likely to be called away by emergencies than if you were available at your office.

Audience

You don't want an audience when you negotiate. Onlookers are partisans—they have loyalties. Negotiators take positions and hold them as much for the audience as for the position itself. They posture for the gallery. They get themselves into corners, where they can't give in without losing face. With friends or associates watching the process, people find it difficult to reach an agreement. Often the posturing is for someone who isn't even present, but someone else is who will report to that person. The likelihood of, and the psychological need for, supportive audiences decreases when you choose a neutral site.

Stacking the Deck

Some adversaries will set up the negotiation room, when under their control, so that they have an advantage.

If the windows admit direct sunlight, such adversaries will take the seats with their backs to the windows and let you squint at the sun. In other instances, they will see you get the seat next to a radiator or a hot-air or cold-air vent. It is petty, but they feel that making you uncomfortable increases the likelihood you will want to get the negotiations over and will more readily accede to their position.

One defense contractor arranges a room so that the chairs of the opponents have legs about an inch shorter than those of the other chairs. Again, it is very petty and is based on the feeling that, by having your opponent look up at you, you create an authority image. This idea is not found only in negotiations. Some attorneys and executives have their desks and chairs on a low platform to help create the authority image. If your opponent uses this technique, you can defuse it by claiming a back problem and standing. Because your opponent believes being higher gives him or her a significant advantage, having you now looking down not only removes the perceived advantage but also creates an air of disadvantage. If opponents believe they are at a disadvantage, then, of course, they are.

The worst case of setting up negotiation rooms we have heard of was cutting the front of the opponent's chair legs 5/8 inch shorter than the rear legs. The effect was simply uncomfortable seating.

A tactic to use against these petty tactics and to gain psychological one-upmanship: after a break, get to the seats first and grab your adversaries' seats. If necessary, slide their briefcases across the table. They will realize you have found out what they were doing and are unlikely to make an issue of the change.

The Prime Seat

People have become used to an authority figure sitting at the head of the table. At home it was likely a parent, and at work it could be a supervisor at the conference table. Consider grabbing the prime seat, preferably facing the door. You are now in the seat of authority. Not only can it have a subliminal effect on your adversary, but it can affect how you view yourself and your power, which is equally important. If there is no chair at the head of the table, move one there. As the person at the head of the table, you can more naturally take charge of the negotiations, even suggesting where the others sit. The authority seat can give you power, even when negotiating on your adversary's home court.

Close, But Not Too Close

When you are more than 5 feet away from a person, you start to be distant; you make it easier for the other party to feel secure in his or her defenses. A distance of 3 to 5 feet is excellent; you don't invade a person's private space but are close enough to establish a physical rapport. When you get your face within about 2 feet of another person's face, you have invaded his space, and your closeness will likely be received as threatening.

Physical closeness tends to make it more difficult to resist persuasion. When you are negotiating in your office, get up from your desk. Take a seat close to the other party. If you need a surface to write on, both of you can use the back side of your desk.

The Kitchen Table

The kitchen table is a great place to negotiate. It provides an informal, nonthreatening environment. Parties are in close contact, and the area is normally well lit. It is the kind of place that is not conducive to role-playing, but to honest discussion and harmony.

The Living Room

While living rooms are comfortable, they are generally poor negotiation sites. The major problem is that the parties are generally too far apart, which is not conducive to reaching an agreement.

Timing Negotiations

When you are dealing with employees of a firm, a good time to set for negotiations or to complete a negotiation is a Friday afternoon or the afternoon before a holiday. Your opponents will likely have weekend plans. They will now have personal reasons for reaching an agreement. You might even suggest that you negotiate the next day (on their time) if you are unable to conclude today. This is especially effective when you have come in from outside the geographical area.

When the other party is coming some distance, schedule negotiations for a Thursday or Friday. The other side will likely want to leave as early as possible because late Friday night flights are difficult to get. Likely he or she has Saturday plans and won't want to be working Saturday morning. Many negotiations go late into the night, but this is seldom the case on Friday nights. By four o'clock a minor concession will likely be received with open arms.

An advantage of afternoon negotiations is that the other party has likely had a big lunch, and possibly a drink or two. This is likely to sap energy levels and lower resistance.

Power Dressing

A plain gold wristwatch and clothes of obvious good quality and taste show power. Power dressing serves to lower the expectations of your opponents. They are unlikely to feel you can be taken advantage of.

While power dressing is a weapon for a seller, many buyers prefer to downplay their wardrobes. It implies that all they can afford is on the table.

Smoking

If you control the place of negotiation, don't put ashtrays on the table if you don't smoke. If your adversary smokes, asking him not to can work to your advantage. In a lengthy negotiation session it can encourage agreement.

If you are a smoker, smoke only if your adversary is smoking. Don't ask a nonsmoker if it is all right to smoke. Out of politeness he or she will likely say yes but will resent you for smoking. You want to be liked in negotiations as much as possible, especially when your adversary is dealing from a position of power.

3. General Negotiation Tactics

Specific tactics (negotiating price, financing, and other issues, and dealing with impasse) are described in Chapters 4–7. This chapter deals with tactics in general.

Tactics are learnable, and their use can be honed by practice. Through practice, you will also discover tactics you are comfortable with. If you are comfortable with a tactic, you will likely use it convincingly; and using it convincingly will lead to successful conclusions.

Arriving Late

When there are several members on your team, a tactic used by some negotiators is to have one member call and state he or she will be just a few minutes late. The purpose of being late (about 15 minutes) is to give other members of the team the opportunity to socialize and break the ice with the opposition. The weaker your position, the more important that you be well liked.

Some negotiators plan on always being about 8 minutes late—not so late that the other side leaves, but enough to be noticed. The purpose is to convey the attitude that we don't really need this agreement—if we did, we would be on time. It is a psychological power move of questionable value.

For the person who likes to keep you waiting, a good tactic is to be close by, but not to appear until your opponent has arrived. If your opponent believes that being late gives negotiation power, you will have given your opponent the perception of having lost power.

Take Charge

By immediately taking control of the negotiations, you can gain a psychological advantage over your adversary. You can accomplish this by starting with, "We will sit over here, and why don't you take the other side of the table?" You then continue with, "Are we ready to begin?" After this, take command of introductions, if needed, and lay out the areas for negotiation and a suggested agenda.

While it helps if you control the negotiation site, a take-charge attitude when you don't tends to neutralize any home-court advantage your adversary might have. Very seldom does an adversary object to your taking charge.

Learn the Names

Exchange business cards or otherwise ascertain the names of all parties. When being introduced, if you repeat the other party's name to yourself three times and try to think of a person you know with the same name, you will greatly improve the chances of getting names straight. A small diagram of the table, with names where people are sitting, will be a quick reminder for you.

If you are unsure of a name's pronunciation, ask; don't just hope you are right. Mispronouncing a person's name is a turnoff.

Whenever you address another party, use a name. It shows respect, and people like to be addressed by name. Using a person's last name tends to depersonalize relationships. Addressing people by their last names makes it easier to hold to an unreasonable position. When this last-name tactic is used against you, you can defuse it by calling the other person by his or her first name and if this doesn't work, state, "We know each other well enough to use first names. Please, call me Bill."

Promises

If you are unwilling to put a commitment down in writing over your signature, don't make the promises during negotiations. It is perfectly all right to be a tough negotiator, but it is never all right to be a dishonest one.

If you deceive, you can expect deception to be used against you. Strange as it seems, people who regularly deceive others are often easy to deceive because they expect others to play by the rules and be honest.

Audience Negotiation

When your opponent has a nonparticipating audience, such as his or her supervisors, let the opponent make his or her points. Let him play to the audience and take strong positions. Don't try to humiliate your opponent; just make a factual presentation. Don't raise your offer or lower your asking price with the audience present. Tell your adversary you want some time to develop a new position. Set up an informal meeting to get additional information and use this meeting to set forth your position and to attempt to reach an agreement. Your opponent can go back to his or her partisans and explain the concessions he or she was able to get, although less than asked for, and both sides can be winners.

Don't Let Personalities Get to You

It is hard to negotiate with a person you find personally repugnant, although that does not mean a favorable agreement is not possible. The natural reaction of many when dealing with an obnoxious person is to harden one's position. If you don't really need the agreement, your opponent's obnoxious nature is going to lead you to an agreement more favorable to you than if he or she were nice and reasonable.

Many people hire attorneys for negotiations. While attorneys provide legal protection, they also tend to carry the adversarial nature of negotiations too far, scoring personal points as well as points on the issues. While having an attorney on your side who is a real S.O.B. can help when you are negotiating from a position of great power, there is a danger it will cost you when you are dealing with a weak hand.

When another party has offended you, the normal reaction is to get revenge. Revenge can take the form of intransigence, which, if the other party wants the deal, will mean getting cleaned out. Try not to personally offend your opponents, and never offend them when they know they are in a power situation.

Attack Ideas, Not People

Avoid the clever personal jabs. You don't want to make points with your ego or your team members; you want to make points with your opponent. If statements don't lay the groundwork for reaching an agreement, don't say them. Try to act professional. It is all right to attack ideas, issues and facts, but never people. When you refer to a position as being "arbitrary," "baseless," "unreasonable," or "asinine," you are not attacking issues you are really attacking people. Many people will take this type of remark personally. A better way would be to state,

> *"If you consider _____, I am certain you will see the rationale in modifying your position."*

Or,

> *"I agree with you in principle; however, . . ."*

In other words, be diplomatic. You may know what the other side is saying, but don't even call it manure. When you squeeze your opponent's ego or damage his self-image, you will more than likely also damage your chances of reaching a reasonable agreement and, if an agreement is reached, your mouth might have cost you thousands of dollars.

Generally, there will be greater antagonisms early in the negotiations than later. An antagonistic position of your opponent could, however, be good news for you, as it is often a defense mechanism when one is dealing from a position of weakness.

If you stray and anger your opponent with a personal remark, or what is viewed as one, apologize at once, explaining your remark was uncalled for and the result of your strong feeling on the issue. You could continue with,

> *"Really, it is the issue that is important—not my unfortunate and uncalled-for remark. Let's work together to resolve the issue to the satisfaction of us both."*

Feigned anger can be a tool to convince your opponent you are serious, but real anger is dangerous and can result in saying something you shouldn't. As a general rule, the more emotional your opponent, the more receptive he or she will be to an emotional appeal.

Their Attacks

Some buyers and sellers actually adopt a bullying approach in negotiations. You can walk away from them, but don't give in to them. If you do, it will only encourage further abuse. Hold firm against the bully until he or she changes tactics.

If the other side makes a negative personal remark, the honest, offended reaction is normally best; it puts the transgressor on the defensive: "I'm very sorry you said that. I have tried to work with you in a completely honest and forthright manner, and now you say something like that. I really think I deserve an apology before we continue." When you ask for an apology, you normally get it, and it will set the other side back several steps in power.

A person with a weak case often uses antagonism as a weapon. If you regard antagonism as a weakness, you take away your opponent's weapon. A good way to treat antagonism is with silence. Your opponent wants you to react, and you fail to do so. After the person vented their aggression and stopped talking a good response would be, "Why exactly do you feel that way?" Sitting close to an antagonistic person makes it more difficult for him/her to maintain the antagonism.

People who accuse you of lying have likely been lying. If your opponent makes such an accusation, you should seriously question any representations that have been made, as well as your desire to continue negotiations.

Show Respect

As previously pointed out, you must completely separate the way you treat the other person's *position* from the person. You must be particularly cognizant of the need to show respect when your adversary is an older person, especially if you are young. Nobody likes a smart ass, especially a young smart ass.

Asking questions and carefully listening to the answers shows that you respect your opponent and are interested in his or her position. Discussing personal interests during breaks can also convey your respect for that person as a person.

Nothing is worse than talking down to a person. Some older people talk down to younger people and vice versa. Men often talk down to women, carefully explaining simple concepts as if they were idiots. Still others take a similar attitude when dealing with members of minority groups. Treating people in a condescending manner only strengthens their resolve to stick it to you if you give them half a chance.

Men tend to use sexual stereotypes in their negotiations. They consider tactics used by women as overly aggressive, but as acceptable strategy if used by another man. If women come on strong, it is a lack of femininity. Men tend to interrupt women more than they do men but also hesitate to argue strongly with women. Such stereotyped attitudes show disrespect for women. A man shows the greatest respect for a woman by treating her like any other opponent—with courtesy, honesty and a firm resolve to reach an acceptable agreement.

Breaking the Ice

When you meet at the negotiation, greet the other party with a firm, dry handshake. If necessary wipe your hands before entering. A clammy hand and/or a weak handshake is viewed by some people as a sign of weakness.

If you are meeting at the opposition's home or office, look for something out of the ordinary, such as an antique in an office of modern furniture, or a trophy, or pictures, especially of pets or objects such as an automobile. Ask a question about the item or picture. If the person is eager to tell you about it, you have hit the right button. Ask more questions; show great interest. Since people like people who like what they like, you will have quickly built the basis of a personal rapport. While you should be interested in what your adversary has to say, you are not going to score any points talking about yourself. Your opponent couldn't care less about your operation, children, grandchildren, pets or possessions.

Ask if you can call your opponent by his or her first name. The answer will invariably be yes, and the ice has been broken. However, don't fawn over people with remarks like "such nice people...," and don't use terms such as "honey" or "dear." These are turnoffs. You will have done just the opposite of what you intended.

Don't tell a joke making fun of anyone. Many people resent this type of humor. If you tell a story about a one-eyed Lithuanian, you can be almost certain your adversary has a glass eye and is of Lithuanian ancestry.

A prominent developer who was born in Poland tells the story about a gentleman who wanted to buy some land the developer was interested in selling. The buyer used an icebreaker, a very crude Polish joke. The developer said this was a million-dollar joke, as this is what it cost the jokester. He made up his mind he wasn't going to sell to this buyer until it became clear his obstinance could be used as a chance to "get the jokester good."

The only one who can get away with an ethnic joke is a member of the ethnic group depicted.

Bilingual

If you and your adversary are fluent in a language other than English, consider negotiating in that language. It adds a closeness and increases the likelihood of an agreement. In a team situation, where you and the chief negotiator on the other team are the only ones fluent in a language, you can often use the language to break an impasse. Simply asking the other party if he or she wants to make a deal quickly—just the two of you. You can then take a break and pound out an agreement without negotiating in front of an audience.

Define the Issue

Make certain before any issue is negotiated that you fully understand what is being negotiated, and make certain the other side also understands. You don't want the seller to tell you, "All right, the price for the building is $_____ and shall be paid as follows: _____.
Now let's discuss the ground lease [or appliances, etc]." In this example the problem was not defined. You have really allowed the negotiated price to be opened again, with the agreement as merely your offering price.

The Impossible Dream

Learn to recognize impossible situations. Don't continue to waste more time because you have already invested too much time. If you concentrate on probabilities rather than possibilities, your negotiation success will improve significantly.

Authority of Opponent

If a seller is alone, without his or her spouse, ascertain if the property is jointly or separately owned. Are there any other partners or co-owners? If your adversary needs the approval of another person, don't negotiate without that person present. Otherwise, you will be making concessions to a person who can't really give you anything in return.

When the other side indicates they have limited authority, an interesting tactic is to claim limited authority as well; if the other side tries for a late concession you can counter it with your own demands.

Your Motivation

The more motivated you are to buy, the more important it becomes that your opponent not be aware of your motivation. When your opponent knows you are in a must-buy mode, you can expect his or her position to harden and few concessions, even minor ones, will be made.

Conduct your dealings in such a manner that your opponent is unaware of your weaknesses. Even if your opponent knows you're in a must-sell or must-lease situation, by acting as if you're dealing from a position of strength rather than weakness you cause your opponent to have doubts about the strength of his or her position. In negotiation, the perception of strength is just as strong a tool as real strength.

The importance of the owner's needs (motivation) at the time of the offer should not be minimized. Recently, a small parcel of land was for sale for $160,000. The owner, who wanted cash, later indicated she probably would have accepted $100,000 for the land. Her financial picture then improved. She was offered $150,000 for the parcel but refused, saying she was no longer interested in selling. The buyer, who owned adjoining property and needed the land for a planned development, finally negotiated a cash sale for $500,000.

Timing

When an owner has had an open house and/or has run an ad over a weekend, a good time to contact that owner is late on a Sunday afternoon. Any owner who has sat at an open house for two days and has had three lookers, two of them neighbors, will be psychologically ready (tired and dejected and likely to listen to reason) for a reasonable offer. His expectations are likely to be significantly lower than at the start of the weekend, and it is an opportune time to negotiate.

When You Are Asked To Make a Purchase Offer

Don't be too anxious to make an offer when you are approached by an owner wanting to sell. Ask questions. Visit the property even if you know it. An immediate offer would show you want the property a great deal and would tend to weaken your power position. Remember, the owner came to you, so you have the power.

Instead of giving the offer you're in a position to make, ask the seller to set a price even if he had an asking price. As a power approach ask for their best price, then counter with your offer.

Don't Recognize Power

If you refuse to recognize that your opponents are in the catbird seat, you lessen your opponents' belief as to their power. You want them to have doubts about their position. Power intimidates many, and when you take an attitude of having power, you can turn the tables to your advantage. The weaker your position, the more confidence you must show. Act friendly but self-assured. Bringing in an assistant or an accountant can aid in your role-playing.

Never assume the other side knows of your lack of power. Even when they tell you they have power, they're not really certain, and you can increase this doubt. One way is to smile. When the other side indicates you must buy from them or sell to them, smiling as if you're about to break out in laughter can be extremely disconcerting. Laughter itself can be used as a weapon because it greatly increases your opponent's self-doubt, giving you phantom power that is every bit as effective as actual power.

Appear confident. It can make the other side doubt their power and re-evaluate their position.

Acting bored during an opponent's presentation is another way to deflate him or her. You undercut the force of the arguments.

A very common problem of negotiators is to overestimate their weaknesses and the other person's strengths. You can use this to your benefit. Repetition of your strengths and the weaknesses of your opponent can result in the ready acceptance of an offer that would normally be rejected immediately. Never underestimate your own power. As long as the other side is talking, they are interested.

Alternatives

Having alternatives gives you negotiation power. A real alternative gives you real power. A phantom alternative gives you the appearance of having power, which can be just as effective as real power if your adversary believes alternatives are available to you.

Don't Show Your Love

As purchaser, never let the seller know you are in love with the property. You will give the seller all your power. Feigning only a mild interest can be effective. Remember O'Henry's "The Ran-

som of Red Chief," where the father's lack of interest quickly reduced the expectations of the kidnappers.

An Enthusiastic Spouse

Treat your spouse as if he or she were a member of your team and
give team instructions not to reveal motivation.

A spouse who falls in love with a property can undermine
any negotiation power you may have, leaving you powerless. If
your spouse says, "I want this house" in the presence of the
seller or seller's agent, your only negotiating strength would be,
"This is all we can afford." If an agent already knows financial
status, this tactic could be lost to you as well.

Consider Their Investment

When your adversaries have invested a great deal of time and
money in your property (engineering reports, etc.) their expen-
ditures will actually improve your position. The more they have
expended, the less they can afford to walk away from an agreement.

Physical Tactics

Eye Contact

Eye contact conveys honesty and interest, but it is hard to look
another party in the eye. A simple solution is to look at the nose.
Don't laugh. It works, and it looks like eye contact.

Body Language

When the other party looks at his watch several times, he either
wants to conclude the deal or get away. If he appears nervous it
could mean the same thing or simply that he needs to use a rest-

room. Suggesting a short break and mentioning where the restrooms are will solve the difficulty. When a party seems anxious to leave, try to close the sale or lease.

A person who crosses his arms and/or sits away from you could be defensive. It normally means you must remove some more ice to reduce the defensive position. Arms closed high over the chest generally indicate a combative attitude, while arms closed lower over the chest signify a defensive position. Open arms indicate sincerity. If a buyer makes what he claims is a final offer and has his arms folded tightly across his chest, it is a good nonverbal signal that the offer is not final. A final offer generally is made with an open, nonprotective gesture.

When you can see your opponent relax, it is an indication that your offer has reached his or her range of acceptability. Now it is time to start holding firm.

Nervous mannerisms are strongly positive indications of a desire to put a deal together (unless, of course, the other party actually wants to leave or needs to use the restroom). The more nervous your opponent, the greater your power and the more demanding you can become.

Wringing hands is a sign that a person is dealing from a position of weakness or perceived weakness.

Leaning forward is an excellent sign of interest, but leaning back is generally a sign of confidence.

Playing with one's glasses or any other object, or stroking the face are signs of contemplation. Be patient and wait for verbal reactions.

If a person makes a statement and remains perfectly still, it is an indication the person is trying to mask any expression. People don't remain expressionless in real life except by conscious effort. It is an excellent clue that the opponent is lying and doesn't want actions to betray the lie or is in a position of weakness. An obvious effort to look you in the eye when your opponent has not previously done so could spell deception.

Some people will actually shake their head no while saying yes. This is an involuntary movement, which is probably more truthful than what has been said.

Keep in mind that nonverbal language is mutual. As you try to read your opponent's nonverbal language, your opponent will endeavor to read what you are really saying with your body.

When you receive clear but conflicting messages from the body language of your opponent, this opponent could be making a deliberate effort to convey a message by false signals but does not realize that he or she is giving other signals unconsciously. Deliberate body signals generally show power when the party giving them believes that he or she lacks power.

Voice

When a person's voice seems hesitant, apprehensive or higher-pitched it usually indicates a trial balloon. The same holds true for *your* voice. When you give positions, don't hesitate. State them as if they were etched in stone. Sound as if what you say is both firm and fair. When asked the key to his success, one well-known negotiator answered, "Sincerity." You must project believability when you say no.

Touching

Touching can bring people together. When people have had a relationship in the past, a two-handed handshake can bring them emotionally closer. An arm on the shoulder is effective when making a confidential statement. However, retreat physically after doing this, so the space is again private.

Whispering

If the other side whispers or passes notes after you've made an offer or concession, suggest that they talk in private. It is generally a good sign, and it usually means you are getting close, although the note could say, "Does this clown think we were born yesterday?"

Thinking

Think before you speak. Don't rush to rebut. Ask yourself what is important. Sometimes it is far better to let the other side feel they have their small debating successes if they are peripheral to the real issue.

Use your break periods to put your ideas into coherent sentences, so you will be prepared when negotiations continue. Taking time to answer questions has another positive side effect. It can scare timid negotiators and often leads to further concessions before you have made your statement.

Questioning

During negotiations, find out as much about your opponent as possible. Needs and motivation will help you in structuring proposals and in setting positions. Your opponent will want similar information. You, however, want the exchange of information to be as one-sided as possible. Don't reveal motivation and needs to the point where your bargaining position will be weakened.

Be very careful what you say about wanting to buy or sell the property. If the seller knows you want it badly, you are like Superman with kryptonite, totally without power.

Ask questions that require detailed answers—not just yes or no. The purpose of questioning is to get as much information as possible. Also, keeping the other side answering questions can weaken their resolve.

Your questions early in the negotiations will help develop proposals that will meet the needs of both you and your adversary:

"What are your feelings about. . .?"

"How long a lease did you have in mind?"

"What exactly are your objections to a triple net lease?"

Keep your questions fairly short. Long questions tend to confuse, and you want to be communicating.

When the other side raises a problem, be very concerned. Ask questions. This nonthreatening approach will help you in formulating solutions.

Blocking

Just as questioning can be used as a negotiation technique, so can blocking, the failure to properly answer questions.

Blocking techniques are used by politicians to answer what they want to answer. For example, President Reagan in conducting his one-minute press conferences as he boarded his helicopter, only heard the questions he wanted to answer. Blocking can be used in negotiations by doing any or all of the following:

1. Ignore the question. If the other side does this, ask again.
2. If the question is a compound question, answer only the part you want to answer.
3. Don't say yes or no if such an answer could weaken your position. Answer instead as if you misconstrued the question and answer it the way you want to. Many negotiators ask good questions but accept lousy answers. They are already thinking of their next question. Be a bulldog if an important question has not been answered; ask again and again until you get your answer.
4. Answer a question with a question.
5. Rule a question out of bounds by saying, "That is an inappropriate question."

Why

When negotiating with little children we very often lose. One reason is the "why" question. By constantly asking, "Why?" they allow us to build our own trap and end up where we just can't answer.

"Why?" works just as well with adults. You can break up the monotony with an occasional "How?" and "Could you explain that again? I really don't understand." You can thus force constant justification. When feelings are expressed, asking "Why do you feel that way?" is very effective.

Objectives of Questions

The question technique allows you to (1) gain information, (2) discover the objectives of the other party, (3) set your own goals, (4) plan strategies to work toward those goals.

During the questioning process, appear interested and receptive to the views of your opponent. You want information. You must not appear to have a preset position.

If you want to relay information to your opponent, try to lead them to ask for it or else provide the information so it appears to be in answer to their inquiry. Volunteered information is less likely to be relied upon fully than information elicited by questioning. Nothing is more frustrating than when your opponent doesn't want to believe the truth.

Listen

Most people know how to talk but not how to listen. Besides what is being said, you should also be alert to what is being implied. This will give you the opportunity to question and clarify. When the other party questions you, your best response is to answer a question with a question. Seldom in a negotiation does an opponent not leave ammunition on the table which will fit your gun. You must listen and question for it.

Don't make assumptions from what is said; ask direct questions and verify the facts, positions and/or needs. By being intent on your opponent's every word and by taking notes, you let your opponent know you are considering what he or she has to say. You want to come across as being interested and fair.

Don't Rush Them

When you seem to be hurrying to an agreement, parties often feel they are being pushed into something. You want the adversary to work for the agreement and feel that pressure tactics were not used.

To do this, rely on questioning to a great extent. Allow the other parties to carefully think through the questions. Give full attention to the answers. Never interrupt your adversary. By agreeing to points made, you show an understanding nature and are more apt to be liked. Being liked is important, as it increases the likelihood of negotiation agreement.

Paraphrase

If you are unsure of the position of your adversary, paraphrase the position according to your understanding and ask if your summary correctly states his or her position.

Explain It to Me

The explain-it-to-me approach asks for help in understanding. It tends to make your adversary relax any defenses because you are asking for help. This approach makes your adversary a teacher and can provide you with a great deal of information. At best, you can have your adversary help you to a reasonable solution.

Keep It Short

People remember the first thing you said and the last thing best. Their memories tend to get hazy about things in the middle. Therefore, keep ideas in digestible doses. Two minutes to present most ideas is adequate. You can then ask questions; the answers will tell you if you got your message across.

Weasel Language

Many negotiators like to use language that allows a change of position. They don't commit themselves until the offer can be presented as a complete package. Instead of "No" they will say, "I don't think I can help in that area," and instead of "Yes," "That is an area for serious consideration."

Really Nice People

Negotiating with really nice sellers can be difficult because they don't want to say anything negative to you even though they might have concerns—about you personally, the financing offered, etc. If you can't overcome these concerns, a reasonable conclusion is not going to be reached. You must question each element of a sale in detail in order to find the concerns. If you fail to understand the problem, you cannot solve it.

Team

When dealing with a single person, try to do so without any help. Bringing in a group can be overwhelming. While some people are more likely to agree when confronted by a united group, more likely they will raise their defenses and no agreement will be reached.

When dealing with a team, having your own team reduces your adversary's perception of power and provides you with psychological support.

Dealing With A Group

When you are negotiating with a group such as the board of directors of a corporation, know which person's interests should concern you primarily. Who carries the clout? The person who answers your questions may be just the motor mouth of the group. Notice whom people glance at when you ask questions. This will usually be the person with the greatest power. While the power will ordinarily go with title (president or chairman of the board), this is not always the case.

Important Person

In a team negotiation, bringing in an important person to conclude the negotiations can be an excellent tactic. It tends to awe the opposition. With a final concession, the important person will likely encounter less resistance than an ordinary mortal. Large defense contractors have brought in retired generals and admirals who are on their payroll to complete negotiations. A charitable institution that had a nationally known entertainer on its board of directors brought in the entertainer to gain a final concession in the negotiations on a site for a new facility. The entertainer's appearance completely awed the seller, and even the attorney for the seller wanted the entertainer's autograph. The result was an agreement.

Japanese Buyers

Because of cultural differences, a few words about Japanese buyers are in order. When dealing with a Japanese buyer, you will often find yourself dealing with a group of people. It is necessary to be polite, and your first step will be an exchange of business cards. Then offer tea and coffee for a nonformal meeting.

When dealing with a group, Americans tend to try to influence the persons who speak the best English. Often, these are the younger members of the group. However, the person or persons likely to have the greatest influence in any decision are usually the oldest persons present.

Some Japanese buyers are slow to explain their exact wishes, so questioning is important. Often, Japanese buyers don't feel it is polite to argue with what you say, so it is often difficult to understand the reaction to your statements.

Because decisions are often made by group concessions, give Japanese negotiators time to meet in private after you have made any proposal.

Many Americans tend to underestimate Japanese in negotiations. At times they appear to pay too much. What we often fail to understand is that the Japanese invest for the long run. Therefore, don't emphasize possible short-term profits in negotiations.

Experts

Don't be overly impressed by experts brought in by your opponent. Consider for a moment lawsuits involving negligence. Both sides generally provide outstanding experts who testify, for fees, to diametrically opposed viewpoints.

Team Questioning

Asking questions directly of the team's weakest members by name tends to weaken the entire team position. When other team members have to come in to reinforce what is said or wasn't said, they will have suffered a psychological setback.

The Snow Job

Some parties attempt to bury you with technical data, especially when their position is weak. When you feel you're being snowed, ask the other side to please put the material in layman's language and explain its relevance to the issues involved.

An Integrity Test

If you are uncertain about the accuracy of information you are receiving from your adversary, ask questions to which you know the answers. If the answers favor your adversary, you know that none of the information provided by this adversary should be fully relied upon in your decision-making.

Your Opponent Lies

If your opponent gives false information don't call him or her a liar, even though you're certain it was deliberate. Say that he or she must have received some misinformation and then provide the corrections. This leaves the door open to completing negotiations. While embarrassing your opponent might give you a great deal of satisfaction, don't do so unless you are prepared to leave.

When you catch an adversary in what you consider intentional deceit, consider how badly you want the deal. Remember that if the party has been dishonest in one area, you can have no faith in any representation made by that party. Analyze your needs and the dangers involved in determining whether you walk away or continue to negotiate.

The Other Side Makes a Mistake

If your opposition provides any fallacious data, you should be very concerned and immediately correct them, even if you believe it was an inadvertent mistake. This will put your adversary on the defensive and you can insist on substantiation of tax figures, utility costs, rents, etc. You have now placed your adversaries in a position where they must prove to you they are honorable.

Fun with Figures

As a general rule, be on your guard when exact, even figures are quoted. There is a high probability they were contrived.

Analyze what the figures actually mean. For example, assume an owner's expenses rise from 10 percent of rent received to 15 percent. The owner could claim his or her expenses have risen 50 percent, which should entitle him or her to a 50 percent increase in rents. While this could sound reasonable, it is nonsense. To keep the same spendable income, the owner needs only a modest 5 percent increase in rents.

A broker might tell you his or her firm has a 25 percent better sales record than the average for the MLS service. If, however, only 32 percent of current listings are being sold during the listing period, then that broker really has a 40 percent success rate. This means his or her listings have a 60 percent likelihood of not being sold. You must understand what the figures mean.

Benefits

In presenting a position, emphasize the benefits it provides to your adversary. You want him to visualize the realities of what you're proposing.

In your negotiations keep in mind that people have needs. You could satisfy the basic needs for shelter, but there are other needs as well—self-esteem, self-actualization, love, belonging, knowledge and understanding. Consider the chance to meet these needs as a benefit offered by the property.

Solving Problems

If there is a problem and you feel you have a solution, the best way to reach an agreement is to let the other side come up with the solution.

Start with a general question such as, "How can we solve...?" Then ask more specific questions, which should lead to the solution. Then combine the answers you received with: "Let me get this straight. What you are saying is if...then we could...."

Help Me

The help-me tactic involves acting so helpless your opponent will feel guilty and go out of his or her way to help you. Shrewd negotiators play like country bumpkins and with apparent honesty claim, "All I have is $____. How can we work this out?"

Guilt can be used as a weapon. It is often used by charities when they negotiate. If they can lay guilt on their opponent, they can walk home with the entire store.

What You Are Bargaining for

During the negotiation process some people lose sight of what they are bargaining for. Winning by getting your way is not winning when you don't need or want to buy (or sell) the property. It is like buying a suit that is way too small for you just because it was on sale. If you don't want or need it, it's no bargain at any price. A deal for a deal's sake rather than for benefits is generally a bad deal.

A Problem

Admitting a problem you realize the other party knows of gives you the appearance of reasonableness. Now discuss possible solutions, and use the best suggestions as a negotiation chip. Don't agree to solve the problem without some concession.

If a problem arises, such as unexpected financing difficulties, don't hide it. Let the other side know. In the long run, honesty will work for you. You can discuss the problem and possibly work out alternatives.

Raise Their Argument

If you know an argument will be used against you, bring it up yourself and defuse it rather than wait to be put on the defensive. Be certain, however, that it will be used, or you could be providing ammunition for your adversary's guns.

I Don't Understand

Foreign buyers at times use a tactic of conveniently not understanding when they don't want to. When your opponent understands your concessions, but little else, realize that the lack of understanding is a tactic. One U.S. developer brought in a Japanese interpreter when the U.S.-educated representative of a Japanese corporation had difficulty understanding his position.

Some negotiators use the tactic of planned stupidity when the other side has made an extremely strong argument. Not understanding can confound the opposition.

The Other Property

When shown a property you really like, a good tactic is to tell the owners you have pretty well decided on another property but you just want to convince yourself it is indeed the best property to meet your needs. Mention features of the property not present in this property but concede it does have several advantages, which you specify. This should set the owners into a selling mode. They have a live one, and they don't want to lose this buyer to another property.

The purpose of this approach is to enable you to make a lower initial offer than could otherwise be made without offending the owners. This offer will reduce the owners' expectations and prepare them for a sale at a significantly lower price than they had hoped for. But, if they sell to you they will be winners, winning out over another property.

If you appear to be rejecting a property, the owners are going to be unhappy. While they may willingly refuse an offer from a buyer who wants the property because the offer is too low, owners don't want their property to lose in a competitive situation against property of another. The less interested you are, the more willing the owners will be to give an attractive price and/or terms.

A similar approach can be used when questioning reveals the property does not have an advantage offered by a competing property. Let the owners' hard-sell succeed and come forth with your low offer.

Don't Knock the Competition

When you are negotiating with a buyer or lessee, he or she may mention competing property in the hopes of establishing power in the negotiations. If you make any comment about competing property at all, it should be mildly positive: "Yes, that's a nice building," or, "A good location." Don't knock the competition; it indicates you want the sale or lease quite badly, and the buyer or lessor will react as if he were dealing from a power position. Keep in mind that if your buyer liked the other property better, he would be in another office dealing with another owner. He is most likely using the other-property technique on you.

You Don't Want It

Your power is greatest when you don't want to buy. If the sellers want to sell to you, they are going to have to include their first-born in the sale as an incentive. The really fantastic bargains are generally made by people who didn't really want the property offered. As your desire to buy increases your power decreases, although a will-buy buyer who is not highly motivated still has a great deal of power. When you do want something badly, you must appear to be a will-buy buyer if you are to have any power in the negotiations.

I've Changed My Mind

When a prospective buyer shows a strong interest in your property, a tactic that can work exceptionally well is to indicate you have been considering withdrawing the property from the market. When you hesitate about selling, the prospective purchaser's primary efforts will be to convince you that you should sell. To do so, the buyer's expectations will have to be adjusted. The buyer will realize a bargain will be unlikely. In other words, you will have redirected the buyer's efforts from hammering your price down to convincing you to sell. When the prospective buyer convinces you to sell, the buyer will be a winner and have less concern about the price.

Yes, Yes, Yes

The "yes" technique simply involves asking a series of questions calling for positive yes answers leading up to the agreement. For example:

"Do you want shoppers with high disposable incomes?"

"Do you want to have the highest foot traffic count in the city in front of your door?"

"Would you like to be between Robinson's and the Broadway, the two highest-volume department stores in the city?"

"Would you like to take advantage of over 15 million dollars in advertising each year by your neighbors?"

"If we [concession], will you be willing to sign this new five-year lease?"

The Spouse

When one spouse is buying without the other, an approach that will make your adversary want to reach agreement before the other spouse gets involved is, "I don't know, my [wife or husband] will probably kill me for buying without [her or him]. [He or she] never seems to like what I like, but I like this, and I'm going to make you an offer without [him or her]. I'll give you. . . ."

Associate with Others

People like to belong. This need can be partially met by pointing out prominent people or people the other party can relate to who have agreed to similar proposals.

The CC&Rs

You can ask an owner for a copy of the CC&Rs (covenants, conditions and restrictions), which are also known as restrictive covenants. Read the restrictions; chances are the owner never has. You will likely find particular restrictions that could be considered negative. When you return the restrictions to the owner, point out the problems you've discovered. By finding items you show concern over, you help to lower owner expectations.

The Radon Test

Radon is a naturally occurring radioactive gaseous element in the soil which has been getting a great deal of publicity. If you are buying a large apartment complex, you should arrange for a test. If the level is on the high side, give the results to the owner. Treating it as a major concern will scare the owner as to his or her liability, which may or may not exist. The net effect is the owner's expectations can be deflated.

While radon has been claimed to be a carcinogen more dangerous than tobacco, we are uncertain at this time as to what the liability of owners will be in structures with high levels of radon.

Asbestos

Most buildings constructed more than 20 years ago have asbestos in them. The cost of removing it can be great, and even when it is removed, the owner can still be liable for its disposal, even when handled by an independent contractor.

Inspection of large structures by a competent engineer will likely reveal asbestos problems. The presence of any asbestos gives the buyer a great deal of power, as its revelation will significantly increase the seller's motivation.

As a warning, before you complete negotiations be sure that you know the extent of the problem and have a good feel for correction costs if correction becomes necessary.

Carrot on a Stick

At the start of negotiations set a date to discuss any other property you might negotiate with your adversary. It can work to your benefit, as he or she can see benefits in a longer-term relationship rather than a single deal.

If an owner has had multiple properties (such as lots) for sale for a period of time, consider an offer on one combined with options on several more. Consider a lower price for the property you are buying and higher prices on the options. Either part of the purchase price can be a consideration, or you can pay several hundred dollars for the option. The net effect should be a lower price for the purchase and a higher price for the option, which you might wish to sell or exercise.

Concessions

Concessions before You Give a Position

Many negotiators strive to have the other side give their position first; then the negotiators question the other side in order to get concessions without giving anything. Don't allow this tactic to be used against you, because it is not bargaining with an adversary; you are really bargaining against yourself with no benefits before you.

Turn Your Offer into a Concession

When the other side sets forth their position first and you question them about their offer, you can make your offer appear to be a significant concession (assuming the other party is unaware of the details). "I am going to have to take a few minutes for a break to change my position. Frankly, I hadn't considered [information supplied from your questioning]. I believe what I've heard will allow me [to make a much higher offer *or* to adjust my sale price significantly]."

They Want a Concession

People want something for their bargaining. Even when they are willing to meet the full price and terms, they could walk away if they can't get a concession. Getting something becomes more a matter of saving face than the value of the purchase. While this attitude does not make economic sense, people are not always economically sensible in their views and actions.

Good-faith bargaining implies concessions, for without concessions it is not bargaining, but a one-price policy.

Offers and Concessions

Always treat an offer as a point to negotiate from, not as a final or firm decision. What the other party presents as a "must" seldom is a "must" as presented.

Accept a *no* as meaning *maybe* and take the position that nothing is sacred. If you don't ask, you will surely never get.

When it's you who is saying no, do so loud and clear. If you do not, *no* or your silence can be taken as a *maybe,* which can become a yes.

Your concessions can often mean what you didn't mean to convey. To another, a concession could be (1) a trial balloon to see the reaction, (2) an invitation to start serious negotiations, (3) a sign of weakness.

Patience

Take your time. Don't rush to give concessions. Don't appear eager. Patience will make your adversaries have doubts as to their power and will tend to reduce their aspirations. Being slow and patient can make the other side lose patience and make the offer or concession.

Silence is a great weapon. It forces the other side to talk; and if they are talking, they are likely to make concessions. When you are not talking, you can't make concessions.

Don't Give Without Getting

If you made the last concession, never make another one without a benefit for the first. By making two concessions in a row, you literally negotiate against yourself—the equivalent of topping your own bid at an auction. Every concession should have a purpose. If there is no purpose, don't make the concession.

Whenever you do make a concession, give your reasons. Cover points made by your adversary. If you don't, your original position will seem arbitrary. In addition, your explanation keeps your adversaries from again bringing up a point. If they do, explain you considered that point in your agreement to accept _____.

Size of Concession

Just because the other side cut the price by $10,000 doesn't mean you should raise your offer by $10,000. This type of reasoning would result in all negotiations ending half-way between initial asking and offering prices. Sellers would ask even more, and buyers would offer even less. Meet a $10,000 concession with a lesser increase of, say, $3,000.

If you give too great a concession or concede too soon, the other side will not believe it's your last concession. They will not be ready to reach an agreement.

Making a significant concession will give some persons the idea you are dealing from a position of weakness, and that other large concessions might be forthcoming if the pressure is kept on. Therefore, consider relatively small concessions to tell the other party you're cutting it tight. As negotiations continue the period between concessions and the size of each concession tends to lessen.

Phantom Concession

Consider asking for personal property of the seller that you would like to have. If you get the property, you will have received the equivalent of a price reduction; if you don't, you have created a demand that can be left as an open issue. This creates a concession that can be given up for a later concession on the part of your adversary. You have really created a phantom issue, but it has value as a concession.

When the other side asks for something you are more than willing to give in to, your hesitancy creates another bargaining chip to be used to purchase real benefits.

The more contingencies an offer contains, the less likelihood of negotiating a major price concession. As a tactic, contingencies can be negotiated and then removed as a major concession for a better price.

Whenever you as a seller intend to leave something with the property because you really don't want it, you should not tell the buyer you intend to leave it. Save this for later and use it as a bargaining chip.

Conditional Concessions

An *if* concession is a conditional concession. "If you were to agree to _____, then I would consider _____." If you don't get the consideration, you don't give the concession. The problem with conditional concessions is you have shown the other side your willingness to give up something which they will now try to get without any concessions, or a lesser concession than asked for.

When the opposition raises the *if* question, they could be simply probing your position and may not be willing to make an agreement as outlined. A better answer than *yes* would be, "If it were offered in that manner, I would certainly consider it. Are you making the offer?"

The Attractive Clincher

Often, an agreement is possible by using a noncash, personal item your adversaries want but would ordinarily not buy for themselves. It should be something that gives them pleasure and can be qualified during small talk before negotiations and during breaks. It can be effectively used in combination with a concession: "All right, now this is it. This is as far as I can go. I'll lower the price $1,500 to $287,500, and if you accept right now I'll throw in my two 40-yard-line season passes for the Bears."

For golfers, the clincher could be custom Ping clubs, for a hunter, a presentation rifle, etc. One builder was showing a young doctor a home in the $500,000 price range. The doctor's wife liked the home, but the doctor was more interested in the builder's restored 1965 Mustang convertible. The builder took out a contract, filled in the price, then laid his car keys on the contract. He handed the doctor the pen and said, "Sign now and the Mustang is yours." He made the sale and lost his Mustang.

Take It or Leave It

When the other side gives a take-it-or-leave-it offer and you are not willing to take it, act as if the choice were never offered. Continue to question and work for further concessions. If the other party continues to answer and listen, then for all practical purposes the choice was not made.

If you identify your offer as final, it is wise to have left room for some minor concessions. People like to get something for their efforts. It makes them feel like winners. Be careful. The final concession after the final offer must be enough to satisfy your opponent, but not so large as to make your adversary feel further concessions are possible. A good time for your final offer is when the other party is getting tired. Consider making your final offer contingent upon an agreement right now. Let the other party know that if your offer is not accepted, you will go back to your previous position. If the other party uses this tactic and you don't accept the offer you should of course consider the final offer as a starting point for negotiation, even though your adversary will be claiming a previous position.

When you state your final position too early, the other side will consider it just another concession and will want to continue bargaining.

I'm Only Authorized to...

This approach is conspiratorial in nature. The other parties indicate they have reached their limit of authority. They take a letter out of their briefcase stating the most they can offer or pay is what they have placed on the table in the form of an offer.

They now tell you they would like a deal and suggest a way to get around the limitation set by their superiors. "If you agree to sell the property for $_____ and I agree to [pay all closing costs, buy the item of personal property for $_____, etc.], we could keep me out of trouble and you could get the equivalent of $_____ more." This approach is often successful because your opponent seemingly comes over to your side to get the most possible from his or her employer. It is dishonest, and it succeeds because of the dishonesty of others. Don't fall into the trap. The limit is imaginary. It was simply a planned tactic.

Whenever a limit is claimed, treat it as a negotiation tactic. Continue as if no limitation were claimed. If you can get the limit crossed, even by a minor concession, you know the limit was a negotiation tactic and it failed.

Surprised and Hurt

When the other party doesn't accept a concession of yours, act as if you are wounded by the refusal and don't understand it: "I am really disappointed that you don't want to accept my offer of $_____. I'm actually hurt you don't feel I am being fair with you. I've tried to be honest in our dealings, and I'm sorry you feel this way." This approach should lead the other party to say they have not questioned your integrity. Ask, "Why don't you think my offer of $_____ is fair?" You should now be very close to an agreement.

One Last Concession

Your opponent has just made a concession, and you feel it's about the best deal you can expect. If there is any little thing you would like, now is the time to get it with, "Throw in ＿＿＿ and let's write it up!"

Don't Push Them

In making an offer if you push for an immediate *yes* or *no,* you will get more *no* responses than you will get *yes.* Generally, a better approach, which gives the impression you view your offer as being worthy of acceptance, is, "I am certain you'll want to discuss this new offer in private. Why don't I leave the room? I'll be ＿＿＿. Please call me when you're ready." This completely nonthreatening approach is effective in getting acceptance or a concession.

Leave It on the Table

When you have made the concession that should have gained acceptance but didn't, a power tactic is to start packing up your papers and state, "I'll leave the offer of $＿＿＿ open until [*give no more than two business days*]. I won't begin any other negotiations until then. If we can reach an agreement on this offer fine, if not, I wish you luck in finding [a buyer or a property]."

This power approach gives the impression of great strength even if you are actually desperately in need of reaching an agreement. At best, you will have an agreement. If you don't hear from the other party, you can find an excuse to contact your adversary again. It should be something like, "I suddenly realized in evaluating [my costs or purchase price] I had failed to consider ＿＿＿."

What If

This can be a creative phase of negotiations, where you present alternatives.

"If I were to handle my own financing."

"If all contingencies were removed."

"If the lease were extended to 8 years."

"If the loan were to be paid off within 5 years."

You're not making a concession, but suggesting different ground rules and asking for an offer based on the new rules. Don't get so caught up in bargaining you neglect to consider alternatives. Options that didn't appear realistic at the start of negotiations might now be the key to an agreement.

If It Were Not for...

When you have a strong argument, it can be far more effective if a proper base for it is established. By questioning you will find specific objectives of your adversary. You can then state, "Am I correct that if it weren't for _____ you would be willing to _____?" This is a rephrasing of what your opponent has said, and if he or she agrees to this premise you then give your argument to overcome the objections. Your adversary can be put into a position where he or she can concede the issue or can back down, thus losing face.

Silence

Greeting an offer or concession with absolute silence and a straight, emotionless face, looking right at your adversary, is a strong weapon. It makes the opponent doubt his or her power and often results in a further concession without a word being spoken.

Silence should also be used if *you* make the offer. You have put the ball in the other court with an offer. Look the other party in the eye and don't say anything until you get your response. Of course, if both sides are using this book as a guide, a staring match will be the result.

When the other side makes a strong point you can't really answer, answer it with silence. It can be very disconcerting to the opposition.

When dealing with a party who greets your offer with silence, you should also maintain silence. Don't retreat from your position. Some people need time to digest ideas.

If you ask a question, wait for the answer. If the answer is not forthcoming, ask again. If you made a proposal calling for acceptance or rejection, keep your mouth closed after the proposal is made. Make the other side respond. The silence can seem deafening, but wait for the answer. If you make a statement, you have let the opposition off the hook.

Inscrutable

Silence and lack of emotion can be excellent tactics if the other side is not sophisticated in negotiations. If you remain inscrutable to the other side's presentation, the other side will reduce their expectations and give up bargaining chips without any concessions on your part.

When the inscrutable approach is used on you, ask questions. Make the other side respond. Questioning tends to eliminate the advantage to anyone using the tactic of inscrutability.

Gather Your Thoughts

When a party has made a particularly strong point, you might want to gather your thoughts before answering. Cleaning your glasses will give you a few moments. Pipe smokers have a great advantage, as tapping, scraping, filling and lighting are lengthy productions and make a person seem to be in deep thought. If you don't have glasses or a pipe, you can gain a few minutes by asking a question for clarification.

Time Limit

Agreements tend to be reached as deadlines approach. Stating a time limit is an excellent technique to help reach a decision. At the beginning of negotiations state your limit, "I have to finish by 6:30 if I'm to make my 8:00 flight." Or, "It's my daughter's birthday, and I have to be home by 4:00." Always try to give a reason for your limit.

Having an ad for an open house in tomorrow's paper acts as a deadline of sorts for a prospective buyer. He knows if he doesn't make a deal today, there's a good possibility of competition tomorrow.

Just as you can set deadlines as a negotiation tool, your adversary can do the same. If a reason for the deadline has not been given, you can generally ignore the deadline as an attempt to force negotiations. Ignoring deadlines also could indicate that the other side perceives you as having the power. If they continue to negotiate after the expiration of their deadline you know you were right, and they have given you even greater power.

When a buyer sets a deadline, ask about an extension. If he is willing to grant one, it indicates a strong desire for the property, which generally translates into a willingness to raise the offer.

When you get an extension, ask for another. The other party will think you're seriously considering acceptance of the offer as written. The time for your counteroffer is just before the extension expires.

When the other side has a real deadline, such as the expiration of an option on adjacent property, you can expect greater concessions as the deadline approaches. In fact, you can probably make your best deal just before the deadline arrives.

Break the Momentum

When a team scores 12 unanswered points in basketball, the coach of the other team asks for a time-out to break the flow. The momentum must be stopped, and time-outs do work. If things are going against you, if you have been surprised by information revealed or you just need time to think things out, ask for a break. It's your chance to reorganize.

Instead of asking for a break to stop the momentum when the other side is on a roll, you can do something as mundane as spilling a glass of water to break up the negotiations. The clean-up process breaks your adversary's monologue, reducing its effectiveness. Your opponent's momentum can also be broken by the defensive tactic of interruption, which can be used to change the direction of the discussion.

Breaking Bread

When the negotiations get rough and the other party has held to what you believe are unreasonable demands, consider breaking for lunch with your opponent without discussing business. Ask questions about the person's interests, family, etc. Just be friendly. This break in the adversarial relationship makes it difficult for your opponent to stay with unreasonable demands. After all, you've broken bread together.

Summarize

Before and after any break, briefly summarize positions. Be absolutely honest, and present the views in an unbiased manner. Ask your adversaries if you have correctly stated their position. This summary process clarifies and gets the negotiations onto the central issues. It also serves to inform. People negotiating are often so busy formulating what they *will* say that they don't hear what *is* said.

Unofficial Lines of Communication

Often, other parties don't believe your limits—considering them merely negotiation ploys. If you haven't been able to get through to an owner that you'll buy another property unless. ., consider informal avenues to negotiation. For example, have an engineer check the property and mention to the manager or owner that he or she doesn't have too much time, as you're having him check [competing property] also. If the owner pumps your engineer for information, he could mention that you won't be buying this property because you can do better on. . . . This method is ethical when honest positions are revealed, but unethical when used to indicate nonexistent competition.

Agents

While most agents treat information received in confidence as confidential, some agents, often new licensees, set aside scruples when a commission is in sight. Therefore, if there is anything you would like your adversary to know, such as alternative properties you're considering, disclosing it to the agent increases the likelihood that your adversary will know of it. Don't, however, let your agent know your lack of power, or the maximum or minimum you will accept. It is not unethical to guard your position against breaches of ethics by others.

Emotion as a Tactic

Emotion can be used as a tactic. One negotiator, who is extremely successful, lets the negotiation get hostile. This gentleman, who has a master's degree in psychology, grows agitated, encouraging his adversary to make a statement he can jump on. He becomes emotional and loud, demanding an apology, which he invariably gets. Suddenly he calms down, and the other party, relieved that he's under control, tends to be conciliatory. It takes a true master of the art of negotiation to work this tactic.

Controlled anger can be effectively used when part of a team. Getting very upset over a statement or action of the other party tends to immediately put them on the defensive. Allowing yourself then to be mollified by a member of your team, who leads with statements to your adversary such as, "Charles didn't really mean that the way it sounded, did you Charles?'' should result in an apology for the real or imagined injury to your sensibilities. This psychological one-upmanship maneuver serves to reduce the demands of your adversary.

When your adversary gets emotional, remain deadpan. Don't make any comments for several minutes. Let your adversary vent his or her real or imaginary anger. When he is finished, ask calmly, ''Why do you feel that way?'' You want to appear reasonable but not defensive. If the anger was a negotiation tactic, your opponent will have suffered an erosion of his or her perceived power.

Often, emotion is not a tactic. Your adversary could be very angry. Keep in mind, however, that people often blow up from a cumulative chain of events, most of which bear little relationship to what apparently triggered the outburst. To many people, a verbal outburst is a catharsis that clears the air for future negotiations.

The Tyrant

The tyrant is a graduate of the John Wayne school of negotiations. There's only right and wrong. What he or she wants is right, and everyone else is wrong. The tyrant takes a hard approach and sticks to it. He or she is a pirate, giving no quarter. Tyrants want the deal their way, as well as the crumbs.

Some tyrants are sadistic; they seem to get their jollies humiliating others. When the tyrant is in a position of power, watch out. Such persons make very few deals, but when they do, the deal is usually one-sided.

The way to deal with a tyrant, short of unconditional surrender, is to try to appear absolutely unreasonable. You must appear to be a bigger S.O.B. than the one you're dealing with. Act as if you had all the power. This is the one time you should talk down to your adversary and even appear to be laughing at him. While not a highly successful tactic, it offers a chance of bringing the tyrant around to a reasonable solution. If the tyrant makes the first concession, chances are you've succeeded.

The reversal tactic can also be used against a tyrant. Suggest two ways to solve a problem—ask for the one you don't want. Your opponent, in order to win, will advocate the other solution. Finally, give in and appear angry, accepting what you wanted all along. This tactic can only be used against a person who wants your total defeat.

What about the Future?

Assume your evaluation of your position is one of extreme power. You feel you have the ability to annihilate and humiliate your opponent, making him or her agree to all your demands some of which may defy reasonableness. You feel your adversary has to give in to you.

In this type of power situation, before you complete negotiations, ask yourself, "Do I want to do business with these people in the future?" If not, your own ideas of morality and business will prevail. If, however, you would like future dealings with these people, you'd better have some consideration for the psyche of your opponent. You want your opponent to feel you respect and even like him (her). You want your position to at least appear to be based on reason. Give something, if only in the matter of terms or clauses.

Reinforce the image that the other person has of himself or herself—a strong, sharp negotiator and an honest person. Also, you want your adversary to like and respect you as an honorable person.

Threats

Threats and coercion should be avoided. If you must use them, be certain the other party has no choice but to agree, and don't plan on ever having any further dealings with this adversary. Memories don't fade easily. If a threat is used, it must be believable; but promises are better than threats.

If you're in a position to pressure your opponent, you don't have to tell him. He already knows it. All your threat will do is to create resentment at best, and hatred at worst.

When They Want To Cut Their Noses Off

At times, parties take positions at odds with their own best interests. You want to discover the why in order to successfully argue against a position not based on logic. Usually it's an emotional problem, and to be successful you must channel the emotional responses away from the sale or lease.

Some negotiators actually use irrational behavior as a technique when they can't justify a strong position. They forget about justification, taking an irrational approach. After awhile, the other side realizes reason will not prevail and either gives in to the demands or forgets the deal.

A tactic used by some practitioners of the irrational approach is to include some plainly silly demands to establish their credentials as weirdos. A weirdo can use the tactics of a tyrant without the resentment.

There's another type of person who takes and holds the unreasonable approaches. These are autocratic people who actually are afraid of a give-and-take environment. They are usually unsure of themselves. You must work on this insecurity by showing the benefits of your position to them.

Bluffing

When bluffing, you must appear sincere. You must appear to have alternatives that will reduce your opponents' perceptions of power. You'd better be able to suffer a loss. Many times, bluffs work; other times, they end in no deal or your having to accede to your adversary's demands.

Change Seats

Consider changing your seating after a break. Taking a different chair tends to throw the other party off pace. While minor, this move can be a cumulative factor contributing to the results.

If your adversaries are several people who are presenting a united front, you can break their physical unity by breaking your team up, sitting on both sides of the table. This forces their team to separate, creating a more informal atmosphere. It becomes more difficult for the adversary team members to derive support from each other. Keep in mind that this can work both ways.

You will notice that people tend to become aligned with their opponent on the same side of the table and against their ally who is now sitting in the traditional adversary's chair across the table.

The Fairness Doctrine

When the other side holds all the aces and knows it, and bluffing is a meaningless exercise, you should appeal to fairness. Get the other party to acknowledge that all he wants is a fair agreement. For example, in renewing a lease for a small store in a mall, you could state: "I'm certain we can agree on a lease that is fair and equitable for both of us. Isn't this what we want, a fair and equitable lease?" When you ask someone if he wants to be fair, it's extremely difficult to answer in the negative, even when he really doesn't want to be fair.

This tactic, while like a broomstick battling a sword, still offers some protection. You can push fairness in the negotiations—questioning proposals based on fairness, making logical-sounding proposals and even agreeing to arbitrate differences. After agreeing to be fair, it's now difficult for your adversary to run roughshod over you.

Don't Give Them Ideas

An offer contingent upon a zoning change to permit a more lucrative use of a property may give the seller the idea that he should change the zoning. Never let a seller know about any of your creative plans for use of a building or lot. This information belongs to you; it is proprietary. Disclosure could result in an owner using your ideas or marketing the property to the highest bidder based on your ideas. Abraham Lincoln said, "A lawyer's time is his stock in trade." The same holds true for creative ideas. Keep them to yourself.

Taking Something Away

If your adversaries want to take something from you in negotiations you've previously been granted, an excellent approach is to open the negotiations by asking for more before they have a chance to make their position known. For example, if you have a property management contract with 7½ percent of the gross as your fee and you have reason to believe the owner is going to ask the fee be adjusted downward to 6 percent, consider asking that it be increased to 8¾ percent because of _____. The best defense is an offense. This way you are not in a wholly defensive mode. By agreeing to keep the fee at 7½ percent, you are able to give your adversary a victory.

Agreements That Disappear

If negotiation can't be completed at one session, don't be surprised when agreements you thought had been reached are opened again for negotiation. Often, people don't do this on purpose; they just remember things in a way that benefits them. One way to minimize this happening is to record what was and was not agreed upon. Play the tape back at the start of the next negotiating session.

Keep in mind, however, that all issues are really open until the final agreement and that you or your opponent can raise issues that were settled earlier. All agreements are really based on a total agreement that has yet to be reached.

Corporate Leases

A representative of a large corporation will likely have great leeway, but some limits, on price. Certain terms, however, may have been set by the corporate attorneys for the negotiator, who cannot modify them. Therefore, place your greatest efforts on the issue of price.

Tenant Shocker

When a commercial lease expires and a tenant wants to continue on a month-to-month basis, or otherwise balks at a new lease or lease extension, the tenant can be shocked into negotiations. The tenant probably feels you need him or her more than he needs you. Call the tenant and simply state you will be bringing someone to see the property at a certain time. (Most leases provide for the right to show the property to contractors, buyers and lessors.) If the people you bring start measuring areas and ask you a great many questions, the tenant's perceived negotiation power will vanish. He or she can now be expected to negotiate in good faith. No representations are necessary.

Bail Out

When you seem to be getting absolutely nowhere in negotiations, a bail-out technique is to slowly collect your material and put it neatly in your briefcase. Get up, put on your coat and move slowly toward the door. The other party will ask where you're going. Your answer: "We don't seem to be getting anyplace. I have the strong suspicion you really don't want to [buy, sell or lease]. Do you?" This usually brings an affirmative answer, in which case you should state, "Then let's get down to business. Will you...?" If you get to the door without being stopped, you should bid the other parties good day and say, "It's too bad we couldn't negotiate. I thought it would have been in your best interests."

The problem with walking out as a technique is you can't use it when you're negotiating at your office.

Which Tactics To Use

We have covered a number of tactics. You can't use all of them in any one negotiation. You should, however, plan your tactics based on the needs of the other party, the subject matter of the negotiations, any problem areas and what you are personally comfortable with. During negotiations you may realize your plan will have to be changed. You must be flexible.

Ethics

If for any reason you would not want to have to face your opponent in the future, you know you have done something wrong and have crossed the line between sharp negotiation tactics and unethical conduct.

4. Negotiating the Price

Some very basic laws of negotiation are:

"If you are willing to pay more, you generally will."

"If you are willing to accept less, you generally will."

Expectations in negotiations are likely to become realities. To be a good negotiator, you must be able to psych yourself up for success. You must believe you will succeed.

Unsolicited Buyer/Seller

When you are approached by an unsolicited buyer or seller, keep in mind that you are in a power position. Don't give a price; make the other side present a price to you. Say, "While the property is not really on the market, I will entertain reasonable offers," or, "While I have not been seeking to buy ____, I would certainly give consideration to a reasonable purchase."

When you receive the unsolicited offer don't rush to counter it. A far better approach is, "Why should I sell to you for $____?" or, "Why should I buy the property for $____?" Make the other side justify the price. Do not give a position, as to do so limits you before you fully understand the other party's motivation. It could be a case where a buyer must have your particular property, which could mean you are in a fantastic power position.

Nervous Offeror

As a general rule, an adversary who seems nervous when making an offer is highly motivated, and the offer made is unlikely to be the top offer.

Keep this in mind when you make offers. Be inscrutable.

Their Position First

Even when you make the initial contact or have solicited buyers or sellers, you want the other party to reveal his or her position before you reveal yours. Again, ask how he or she arrived at it. Learn as much as you can about your adversary's position before you reveal yours. Discovery is an important part of negotiation. Your questioning could result in your opponent making an adjustment in your favor without the necessity of exchanging benefits. You can solicit such adjustments with a simple, "What is your best price?" Even though your adversary has modified his or her position in your favor, don't assume it's the best price you will get.

By questioning, you can determine if your adversary's position is based on intrinsic or external factors. If intrinsic to the property, you want to convince your adversary of the merit of your offer. If, however, the position is external to the property, such as a need for a particular dollar amount for some other purpose, chances are you must develop alternative solutions to meet your adversary's needs. Otherwise, you will be unable to negotiate the price. Alternative solutions include financing for your adversary's needs.

When a seller asks more than you anticipated or a buyer opens with a lower figure, don't adjust your position based on the offer made. Unsophisticated negotiators often make immediate adjustments, offering more than they had originally intended or lowering their asking price based on the offer of the other party. They do this so the difference in positions will not be as great. If you do this, the other party will be the winner. He will have gained a concession in your original offer.

A very high initial sale price and a very low initial offer is generally the attempt by one party to lower the expectations of the other. People really don't expect unreasonable offers to be accepted. There are times when you will want to adjust your initial position before you give it, which is a strong reason for having the other side present its position first. If a seller asks less than you expected, lowering the initial offer would be in order.

The Great Initial Offer

When an initial offer to buy is more than your minimum sale price or an initial offer to sell is far less than you were willing to pay, the temptation is strong for an immediate full acceptance.

There is a major problem with agreeing too fast to an offer. The other party will often have second thoughts, believing he should have offered to buy for less or offered to sell for more. While you want a quick agreement, you also want one that will be honored. In this type of situation, you should immediately commence negotiations but try for concessions. If you can't get major concessions, try for a minor one. You don't want the other party to have second thoughts. In this manner not only will the contract be signed but it will likely be honored.

When agreements are reached very quickly, it usually means you came out very well or very badly. You either lacked knowledge or had superior knowledge of the facts.

Setting Your Initial Offer

In deciding on your initial offer, besides the value you place on the property, consider motivation of seller (or buyer), how long the property has been on the market, other offers and why they were not accepted or failed, as well as your alternatives and those of your adversary. You also should realize there must be some room in your initial position to allow for your adversary's bargaining. The lower your offering price or the higher your asking price, the more room you have to maneuver.

Your initial position should have some basis, so you don't have to retreat immediately from it upon questioning. You want to be able to hold your position until you have obtained significant concessions from your opponent. Then, of course, you want to give as little as possible. Keep in mind the best and friendliest negotiation is still an adversarial relationship.

Present your initial position not as a trial balloon but as if you expect it to be accepted. When it is not, question the other party about why it wasn't. To emphasize benefits, you might say, "Perhaps you didn't fully understand my proposal. This is a cash offer with no contingencies."

Being totally honest in negotiations can be disastrous. If you were to make an initial offer based on your best position, the most you would pay or the least you would accept, you will not please your adversaries. Seeming intransigent makes your opponents feel thwarted by not being able to realize any benefits from their negotiation efforts. The inability to save face by obtaining concessions could even lead to the rejection of offers that are in your adversary's best interests. Many sellers are actually more pleased to sell at $100,000, when your first offer was $70,000, than if you had met their $110,000 offering price. By starting at $70,000, you allowed them to gain $30,000 during negotiations. If you had met their asking price, they would not have had the satisfaction of the gain. Offering more than is needed or accepting less than could be received isn't going to make a happy adversary, nor is it good business for you.

Presenting Price

If you are a buyer, before you present your price, give a summation of alternative properties you are interested in that have features this property does not, prices of comparable properties and their features, problems concerning the property being negotiated, and your rationale for your offer.

If you are a seller, give the basis for your price, such as land values, construction costs, income and comparable recent sales.

Understanding Positions

As a seller you have a position. You might want to receive $500,000 for a property, but you might have set a minimum acceptable sale price of $425,000. The buyer might have a position also with the intent to offer $375,000, but he or she might be willing to go up to $450,000. Expressed schematically:

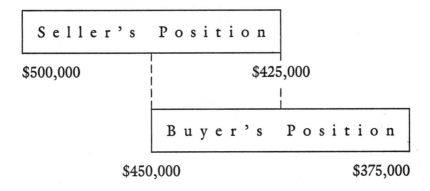

From the initial facts, it seems that negotiations would surely result in an agreement somewhere between $425,000 (the seller's minimum sale price) and $450,000 (the buyer's maximum purchase price). What actually happens is that during negotiation expectations of the parties change, and there can be either a greater area of overlap of possible agreement or complete separation where agreement is not possible without a position change. Because neither party knows the true position of the other, negotiation skills become very important—the buyer trying to purchase at the lower edge of the seller's sale position and the seller trying to get the buyer to pay as close to his or her maximum price as possible.

Bluffs sometimes work and other times result in a party believing a position will not be altered. When this happens at a price outside his or her range, that party might seek another buyer or seller; and a sale which should have taken place does not.

As a general rule even a seller who is desperate tends to raise his or her bottom line as soon as an offer is received. Generally, the bottom line of sellers tends to go down as the time on the market increases (assuming there is some seller motivation other than just profit). Therefore, negotiations are usually more fruitful to the buyer when negotiating with a seller who has had the property on the market a long time.

Never indicate to an opposition your position is a range. If you give a range to your opponent, it isn't a range but the highest price you will pay or the lowest at which you will sell.

Planned Retreat

While normally we advocate taking an initial position which can be defended and held until concessions are given by the other party, there is a technique where everything is done in contravention to the rules. In this technique a seller sets a completely unrealistic price, making a quick retreat without concessions from the other side, then makes a second retreat, cutting the price even further. He then stands pat and refuses to budge. A variation of this is the seller giving one price and before he or she is even through giving a significantly different price. When this difference is pointed out, the seller appears flustered and agrees to the lower price, which he lowers again during questioning. This approach gives the other party the impression the seller is very unsophisticated, has set the asking price too high, and has now changed to the low-dollar figure. From this point on, if concessions are possible, they will be minor. This is exactly what the sophisticated seller wants to convey. By this role-playing, the buyer almost feels sorry for the mistake, and after holding firm the seller says something like, "If you will sign the purchase agreement right now for $_____ [a further reduction], we can have a deal, but I won't extend this offer. I've already reduced the price far more than I should have."

The One-Price Seller

A price in a sales brochure seems to give legitimacy to that price. Because it appears to be a price that cannot be negotiated doesn't mean negotiations are not possible. Even large tract builders who have what appears to be a one-price policy often negotiate prices on appliances and additional extras such as patio slabs. Keep in mind that builders want to appear to have a one-price policy so they don't encounter difficulties with other owners and buyers, but they often are strongly motivated to sell. What is important is the basic price for the house and standard extras. Nonstandard items are often wide open for negotiations, which could be significant.

"I Can't Guarantee the Price After..."

This statement, often used by land salespersons and builders, implies a price increase is forthcoming. This unethical approach creates a false sense of urgency.

The Price Is Too High

If the other side quotes a price that is too high let them know. Don't beat about the bush with minor matters first. This can tend to raise their expectations.

When the other side claims your price is too high, ask, "By how much?" This really makes them give an offer.

When given an offer, you should ask, "Why?" making them justify the price. Your position should be, "All I want is to be fair."

When you're attacking the price of another, of course, you want the offeror on the defensive, justifying the price by explaining how he arrived at it.

You as a Nice Buyer

If you come across as a really nice person, an owner will be less likely to get angry with a low offer. You could say something like, "I really love your home. I would be more than willing to pay any price for it, if I could. But the reality is I am going to have to spend at least $_____ on _____. I am stretching my budget with the offer I'm going to make, but it's all I can afford."

The all-I-can-afford approach points out problems with the property but doesn't denigrate it or antagonize the owner. With this approach the owners, hopefully, will want to figure out a way for you to own their home.

"That's All I Can Afford"

A variation of the above is the "gee whiz!" "Honest!" approach where you agree the property is probably worth a great deal more and if the sellers wait long enough there's a good chance a buyer will come along and pay more. However, with the offer of $_____ and the financing you are stretching your resources to the breaking point. You are not knocking the property but point out it could be a long time until they get more money. This approach is really a take-it-or-leave-it proposition phrased in a manner less likely to result in resentment.

When the seller asks for a greater down payment but you feel he will accept less, a sometimes effective tactic is to take out a bank deposit book, lay it on the table, and say, "That's what I have to work with."

When the "that's-all-I-have" approach is used on you, consider tailoring an offer with a deferred down payment or longer repayment period. Because of the ability to tailor sales to meet particular needs of others, this approach can backfire.

Value

People will pay based not on value but on what they perceive the value to be. In negotiations as a seller you strive to increase this perception conversely; sellers will sell based on what they feel is fair to them. In negotiations as a buyer, you want to decrease that perception as much as possible.

The Appraisal

If the opposition quotes an appraisal, ask if you can see a copy of it. If they can't supply one, chances are it was a tactic to deceive you and no such appraisal exists.

You should realize that a great many appraisals are worthless. There are too many so-called appraisers who will sign their names to anything. At best, an appraisal is merely an opinion of one person at one particular time.

If the appraiser's qualifications and professional designation are not included in the appraisal, consider it worthless. Designations that indicate ability include MAI, RM and SREA. Several appraisal organizations literally sell their professional designations, requiring only a self-serving statement from the applicant as to having met the standards.

Comparables

As a buyer, you want to emphasize the lowest-priced sale of a comparable property without regard to terms of sale. As a seller, you want to emphasize the highest-priced sale of a comparable property. Either way, you want to know the terms of the comparable sale cited by your opponent, as this knowledge can be used to show that the comparable is unrealistic because of the difference in financing.

Having data on a recent sale and a picture of the property is an extremely strong argument for accepting a similar price.

Offer the Appraisal

With this approach, you obtain a fee appraisal on the property. You could then state, "I'm willing to pay the fair market value for the property; are you willing to sell for the fair market value?" To say no, your adversary would be forced into a position of saying he or she doesn't want to be fair, so a positive reaction can be expected. Continue with, "I have engaged Seymour Hopkins, who is an independent fee appraiser with the MAI designation. Here is the appraisal. I'm willing to pay the fair market value indicated. Are you willing to accept it?" Then hand over the appraisal. Make your adversary read the evaluation. Don't make any comment at all. The ball is now in your adversary's court.

Agree To Arbitrate

A tactic that smacks of fairness is to agree to arbitrate. Consider as one of the ground rules the requirement that the arbitrator choose the closest price (yours or your opponent's) to the price he or she determines.

A variation of this approach is that buyer and seller write down the same or a new position, which will be the prices considered by the arbitrator. Most parties will give a little with this approach, wanting to increase their chances of winning at arbitration. The result frequently is much closer positions and a split-the-difference solution.

Lists of arbitrators who can be used are available from the American Arbitration Association and the Federal Mediation and Conciliation Service. A simple method of choosing an arbitrator is to take ten or twenty names off the top of the roster and have each party eliminate one arbitrator in turn until only one name is left. Arbitration fees run from $250 to about $700 per day, plus expenses. The parties generally split the arbitration costs.

Does It Include...?

During your discussion you can ask if the sale price includes items such as appliances, furniture, etc. The sellers, in hopes of a sale, will often include one or more items even when they had not previously considered doing so. Now, ask what they think _____ is worth. Since they have agreed to give the item, they will likely set values high. When the seller concedes to what you believe will be the last concession, you can now state,

> *"Mr. [Ms] _____, at $_____ we have a deal. It was a hard negotiation, however there will have to be a few minor adjustments. I don't really need _____. You indicated a value of $_____ for _____. We'll use that figure and simply deduct $_____ from the price making it $_____."*

Your opponent has been hoisted on his or her own petard.

The Fisherman Approach

Several years ago a large five-year-old condominium project in California had several hundred resales on the market. The market was soft with few buyers. Most of the units were priced from $135,000 to $160,000. The fee sales had been in the $125,000 range for unfurnished units. A buyer went to a local broker and looked at several units. She then wanted a list of all of the particular units she liked which were available through multiple listing. She wrote up over 30 offers for $100,000 cash for each of the units, giving the order of presentation based on further showings. She gave a cashier's check to the broker for $20,000 made out to an escrow, with instructions that it not be deposited until an offer was accepted. She clearly indicated she would not consider counteroffers and that, upon rejection of an offer or failure to accept within the 24-hour period specified, the next offer should be made. She instructed the broker when presenting an offer to tell the owners of the other offers. She had six rejections before she made her purchase.

This approach was beautiful for that particular market. Owners knew they had a chance but had to make up their minds quickly. As an alternative to acceptance, they would be risking waiting several years to sell, when the interest payments would effectively eliminate a higher price. By casting out enough lures, she was able to catch her prize.

Get the Combined Price

When a seller has a number of properties, such as lots, a technique that is very effective for a quick agreement is to ask: "What is your best price for all three lots? All right, I'll take lot 7 at [one-third the price quoted]." The seller will likely object, as the price quoted was for all three lots, but will usually agree.

But I've Already Reduced the Price

Sellers look at a prior downward price adjustment as a price reduction, something they have given up. You must educate them that lowering the asking price is not giving anything up. Arguments such as the following can be used: "Mr. Jones, how long have you had the property on the market at [higher price]? How many offers did you receive at that price? Mr. Jones, you as a seller don't really set the price. The market sets the price. Have you ever invested in stocks? If you wanted to sell a stock and gave your broker a price above market, it just won't sell, isn't that correct? People don't pay more than the market value. You had the property for sale at $\_\_\_\_$, and you have now reduced it to $\_\_\_\_$. The reason you did this is because it didn't sell at $\_\_\_\_$. Isn't that correct? You were not lowering a price, something you had, you were setting a new price closer to what you believed the market would pay. Isn't that correct?''

Hold Your Position

Generally, you want to hold a position as long as possible. Try to appear open-minded, but say that you just see no reason to sell for less than what you believe is fair value or pay more than fair value. You want to voice the words of reason while letting the opposition's reasons for change roll off your back. When you do make a concession, the other parties will really appreciate it because they have worked so hard for it.

If your adversary tries to get you to reduce a price by some argument such as, ''You won't have to spend $4,000 on points with this offer, so it really should be $96,000, not $100,000,'' your response could be, ''Are you offering $96,000?''

Another way to treat an argument for a specific reduction is to state, ''You're a tough bargainer, but we have a deal. I accept your offer of $96,000.'' Your adversary, who only wanted you to reduce your price, is suddenly nonplussed. At worst, he will retreat in embarrassment, and at best you have a deal.

Putting a Price Difference in Perspective

A major difference between your offering price and what the owner wants can lead to personal animosity on the part of the owner. A simple statement that can defuse personal feelings is: ''I don't decide what your property is worth. The market makes that decision. While the market will dictate to me not to pay more than the market value, you as a seller will be influenced by the market not to accept one dime less than the market value. That's the way it should be. Our disagreement really boils down to what is the market value. Mr. Jones, what is the basis for your value of $_____?'' This very reasonable-sounding statement indicates a truly reasonable approach on your part, and asking for justification of a price smacks of reasonableness.

You Will Pay Points

If you will be paying points to get new financing, this can be important in negotiation. Assume you will have to pay three points (three percent of the loan) to get your financing, a $200,000 loan. Your costs will be $6,000. When you make your offer, let the seller know your $245,000 offer is really $251,000 since $6,000 is going to the lender in points. It is identical to paying the seller $251,000 and having the seller pay your points (in fact you could suggest this as an alternative). The seller will now realize he is getting over $250,000, not the $245,000 you are offering. The fact that you are paying this amount can be almost as important as his getting it. He may complain that the lender is taking too much, but you have shown you are paying $251,000 for the property. You can even consider raising the offer by all of your closing costs, including title insurance, lender appraisal fees, credit report costs, etc., if the seller pays them. This can be important when the seller has a price in mind. You thus show you are paying the price, although the seller isn't receiving it.

Writing It Down

In negotiations, writing a purchase figure down on a piece of paper has a greater psychological effect than giving a verbal offer: "I'm afraid we are still apart, but here is the best I can do." Write the figure down and hand it, written side down, to your adversary.

Minimum or Maximum Price

It is all right to ask the other side for the bottom or top dollar price, as it will often result in a price adjustment in your favor.

But when the other side asks this of you, the best response is, "Why, don't you think $_____ is fair?" You have hit the ball back without the other side making a point.

The Chiseler

When you have quoted a fair selling price and you feel the other side knows it but is still trying to get you down a bit more, a good tactic to use (after a break) is to say, "Perhaps we should put off these negotiations. It's obvious my price is too high for you, and I'm having second thoughts about selling anyway. My wife loves the neighborhood, the schools are excellent and the house really is as close to perfect as we could hope to find."

Buyers like to be the ones who decide not to buy. They don't like you telling them the deal is off. The result should be that the buyer will pay the price, as being able to buy becomes more important than a price reduction.

A similar tactic is, after a break, to announce that you must withdraw your last offer because you forgot to consider _____. Now make a new offer several thousand dollars higher. The chiseler will now be trying to get you down to your old price. One custom builder will never come down to the old price. He gets great pleasure in making the chiseler pay. The tactic is extremely effective.

There is a difference between being a chiseler and using good negotiation strategy. One difference: when the other party does it, it's chiseling; when you do it, it's strategy.

Zero Coupon Bonds

While zero coupon bonds are normally used by purchasers (see Chapter 5), they can be used by sellers in a completely different manner. Instead of discounting the price, a seller can offer to return the entire purchase price. For example, for a $180,000 sale the cost of a $180,000 zero coupon bond due in 30 years would be approximately $12,000, based on a 10 percent yield. The idea of getting back everything you paid when the loan is paid up (in 30 years) provides an attractive alternative for negotiations: "How would you like to be given back every dime you pay for this property plus get to keep the property as well? Does it sound too good to be true? Well, let me explain."

Burn Your Bridges

The other side must believe your price is as low as you will accept or as high as you will pay. You can convince them by burning your bridges behind you. With this tactic, you lose the option of retreat, but it strengthens your position.

An example of burning bridges is a corporate officer declaring to the board of directors or stockholders that he will not sell or buy at less or more than a stated price. The other side realizes he now cannot sell for less or pay more than a stated amount without a complete loss of face.

Before you burn your bridges, be certain of your power in the negotiation. It's a dangerous tactic, but very effective if you properly evaluate your power.

Your Bottom Line

Don't rush to arrive at your bottom line. Your bottom-line position is one of last resort. You must firm up before then so that it is clear that here is where you'll make your stand. If the other party believes there is more room for you to negotiate, the result will be impasse.

They Are in Your Ballpark

When the other side have made their position one you can agree with, don't jump to do so. When you agree too quickly to a concession, the other party will feel he gave away too much. Continue to negotiate for more. Now every further concession is really money in the bank for you.

The Minor Difference

Don't lose a deal for peanuts. If it's a worthwhile deal, it is worth a minor concession to make it. Often, pride won't allow a seller to make a small concession and pride won't allow a buyer to buy without the concession. An old Russian saying, roughly translated, is, "Don't quibble over the kopecks; you can make it back with rubles."

Raising Your Price

You can raise your price as seller anytime before final agreement. When the buyer insists on what you feel are unreasonable price reductions, consider raising your price above your last offer. Don't appear arbitrary. Provide a logical reason for the change in your position. You can then use the *if* approach: "If you would agree to offer $[the former price], I would agree to give serious consideration to it."

The effect of going up in price is to drastically lower the buyer's aspirations. When used against you, keep in mind it is most likely a tactic. The seller will reduce the price, even if it appears firm, and further concessions are still possible, but you are probably approaching the bottom limit of an acceptable sales price.

The other side of raising a price or retracting an offer is that it is viewed by many as being against the rules. It can result in the other side toughening up or walking out.

Some negotiators will open negotiations with a new higher price. Again, the purpose is to lower expectations and to reach an agreement in the area of the original price.

In team negotiations, when the other side changes position and takes back what they have given, it is a good time to change negotiators. The new negotiator should now start from scratch. You should take the position that, by reneging, they really wanted to start over.

Splitting the Difference

When your adversary claims to have made a final offer that you consider reasonable, make your own final offer and try to get your adversary to agree to it. We now have two final positions, and it's time to split the difference (see Chapter 7).

Cash Can Hypnotize

A very successful dealer checks out the title before he meets with the owner. If it's free and clear he prepares all documentation, including a deed, in advance. He also has a notary public available.

His tactic after questioning the owners is to get the owners to name a price, which he then attempts to undermine with comparables and facts. He then opens a briefcase and slowly begins taking out $100 bills. He doesn't say a word and doesn't appear to be counting, but he knows what he's putting on the table. Taking out a purchase contract, he writes in the price and hands the contract and pen to the owners. The owners can't get their eyes off the pile of money that is theirs for a signature. If the buyer has to pay more, he lays out more $100 bills. This has been a highly effective tool for this purchaser. It should be pointed out, however, it is only effective for property owned free and clear and you're absolutely certain the title you will get is marketable and/or insurable.

There are a number of other ways buyers use cash to persuade sellers. One buyer purchases foreclosures from savings and loan institutions. When the lending officer smiles at the offer with the obvious meaning of "You are rather naive if you think we would accept such an offer," the buyer opens his briefcase and starts setting packages of $100 bills on the desk. He lays out the entire purchase price. What was a few minutes ago an offer to be immediately rejected now usually ends up with a call to one of the vice presidents or the president. The buyer in this case has found lenders want out of foreclosed real estate and they would just as soon let someone else handle the paper after being burned. They have also seen buyers fail to be able to come up with cash and/or financing. A positive, quick sale is a very strong argument.

Whoops!

If you offered more than you should have or think you might have gone too far, ask for a break. Reevaluate your position. If you can live with your offer, let it stand. If you can't, first consider if other concessions would allow you to keep the offer open. If not, you will have to retract your offer. In doing so, explain your reasons and apologize.

When you retract from a position which you can't later agree to, you significantly reduce any chance of agreement. Chances can be enhanced somewhat if you give other concessions at the time of retraction.

Auctions

Besides foreclosures and tax sales, auctions are increasingly being used as a real estate marketing tool. Auctions are pure price negotiations, as all other terms have generally been set. Unlike other negotiations, you are not negotiating with a seller, but rather with other buyers.

An auction involves some role-playing. You want to appear calm and self assured. If you look nervous, it will be a clue to the experienced auction investor that you are close to your limit and are unlikely to remain in serious contention. You want to make others think you are serious competition so they either drop out from bidding or fail to bid. You can accomplish this in a number of ways.

An auctioneer might set a minimum bid. Bids then progress in small increments until there are only a few bidders left. These bidders will then raise the ante. For example, instead of boosting the bid by hundreds of dollars, they will boost it by thousands to scare there opposition. It is an excellent tactic, but it can actually be used earlier in the bidding. An initial bid significantly above the minimum price will cause many hesitant bidders to abandon their hopes of stealing the property. If the bid is topped, it is unlikely the other bid will be significantly higher. If you again bid, raising the ante several times greater than the raise to your initial bid, you have a good chance of scaring off the opposition. It is important to remember that increases in bids that are not significant keep your opposition in the game.

Heavy bidder strategy can also be used by staying out of the initial slow bidding. The psychological effect of a later bidder coming in as a heavy hitter can effectively knock out the competition.

Developers frequently hold auctions to dispose of large numbers of unsold condominium units or homes. In such a case pay attention to the crowd. There will be both individual buyers who want a unit to live in and investors. A clue to help you distinguish the two is that seldom will a person buying a unit to live in be at the auction without a spouse or a close friend. Investors often arrive alone. Normally, at such a sale the first few units sell at premium prices to people who want them for homes. Pay attention when the people you regard as investors drop out of the bidding. After a while, prices begin to fall, with investors obtaining units. There will be individual units, however, that sell for higher prices due to a desire for that particular unit by a noninvestor. The prices that investors are paying, after the initial price drop, could be close to the bottom of the range. The lower prices actually encourage hesitant investors and people looking for homes, so that the prices may again rise. If the rise in price occurs before the majority of units are sold, it is likely to peter out and the last units will probably sell at an even lower price than the initial one. If, however, the prices start rising when 25 percent or less of the units remain for sale, the last units sold are likely to sell at a premium.

Lease Renewals or Extensions

A tenant whose lease is up wants to obtain a new one with the same or better terms. What he or she will pay is based on comparables—not what similar property is renting for but rather what it will take to rent comparable vacant property. A lessor is not in competition with rented property, only with vacant property.

Actually, a commercial tenant in possession will pay more than what it would cost to rent a comparable property. The lessor has the power to negotiate a higher rental because, to relocate, a tenant would have to pay the costs of moving, phone installation, redecorating and/or remodeling, stationery, new signs, business lost during the move, inconvenience to customers, etc. It is not unusual for a lessor to negotiate a new rent 10 percent higher than rent for comparable space because the lessor is negotiating from a position of power.

When a tenant moves, the lessor has a period of lost rent, costs to rerent, plus likely redecorating and/or remodeling expenses. The rent paid by any new tenant would unlikely exceed what the current tenant could rent comparable space for. Because of the cost of a vacancy, especially if it would cause a negative cash flow for a financially weak owner, a tenant could conceivably negotiate a new lease at less than the cost of comparable vacant space. To do so, the tenant must appear to the landlord to be negotiating from a position of power.

By asking about additional space when he knows it is not available, the tenant is conveying that he has outgrown the location. Explaining to the lessor that a new location would offer advantages reduces the owner's aspirations about asking for an above-market rental while retaining the tenant. Again, the perception of power is every bit as important as power itself.

Renegotiation of Leases

A tenant may want to renegotiate an existing lease. If a tenant claims he will go bankrupt unless he gets a lower rent, make your decision based on the marketplace. If there are few vacancies, you would be ahead by refusing to give the lower rent but letting the tenant assign his or her lease to a new tenant. Consider the chances of rerenting when there are many vacancies. Also, verify the tenant's need for lower rent. If it isn't just a negotiation tactic, he should agree to let your accountant check his books.

If the tenant needs a lower rent to survive and you don't want to lose the tenant, offer to defer part of the rent until the lease expires. If the firm survives and you want a new lease, the deferred rent due gives you extreme power to obtain whatever you want in the new lease.

Due to some long-term leases lagging behind inflation, some tenants are getting bargain rents. It is possible for a lessor to get the tenant to agree to a significant rent increase prior to expiration of a lease. While a tenant would not normally consider paying more than he is required, there are times when he or she literally must agree to do so.

If a location is exceptionally good or if the tenant made significant permanent improvements and is prospering, a tactic used by some property managers is to ask a major competitor of the tenant if he is interested in competitively bidding for the site. Tell the competitor he would have to agree to a lease that starts when the current lease expires, such as in two years. Then explain that the lease will not become effective if the current tenant renegotiates the present lease within 60 days. While the competitor realizes he is being used, he still understand he has a chance at a choice location, and any chance is better than no chance. After the lease is negotiated, the property manager approaches the tenant, shows the lease and asks if he wants to renegotiate the lease with the new rent, effective immediately (in some cases retroactive to the first of the year). The lease is a fait accompli, and the tenant is dealing from a position of weakness. The result is a new lease effective immediately at a reasonable rent.

New Leases

As a lessor, you should try for a higher rent, even if it means concessions such as free rent or premiums like a new color television or paying the tenant's moving expenses. The reason for the higher rent is that a tenant is more likely to remain for a lease renewal with high rent than is a tenant with a lower initial rent (without concessions) now raised to the higher rent.

An additional reason for above-market rent coupled with concessions is the danger of rent control. If rent control goes into effect, the base rent would be the rent being received. The lessor with the above-market rent balanced with concessions will have the advantage.

Rent Schedules

Rents take on legitimacy by simply being printed in a rent schedule. Having other tenants on the schedule gives additional legitimacy to the rents as printed.

Raising Rents

Try to time rent increases with any renovations, improvements or repairs you have planned. Tenants will be more receptive to higher rents if it appears they'll be getting something for the extra money.

Construction Contracts

Just because you ask for bids doesn't mean you will award a contract based on low bid. You can negotiate with several bidders.

Construction price alone should not be the basis for contracting. You want a contractor of integrity and financial strength who can and will live up to any agreements reached. You can use one contractor's lower bid to negotiate a contract with a contractor you feel more comfortable with.

There is a danger of negotiating price too well on construction contracts. Contractors will often be overly optimistic and accept contracts where they lose money. In the absence of great financial strength or a performance bond, the result can be a half-finished project with liens and additional time and dollars to get the project completed.

Change-orders are the rule rather than the exception in large commercial structures. These changes, some major but most minor, run into hundreds or thousands of dollars. On a change-order negotiation the prime contractor is generally a sole-source contractor. As such, the contractor is negotiating price from a position of great strength. Many contractors bid close on the construction contract feeling they can make their profit on the change-orders.

If you are negotiating a change-order you have the choice of agreeing with the contractor paying his or her price, or make the modifications after completion. When the changes can be made after completion you have negotiating power, if they can't you're without power.

You can appear to have power if you ask for prices on a number of items, some of which you don't want. You should then meet with the contractor. Negotiate items you don't want first. When the contractor gives you the lowest price, tell him you feel it's not worth it and that you won't go ahead with the changes. Now the contractor will, hopefully, feel the changes you want are discretionary—not mandatory. When you don't have to have something, you're in a position of power.

If at all possible, avoid a cost-plus-fee construction contract or modification. You're inviting inefficiency at best and dishonesty at worst. A fixed price, even if high, is normally preferable to any cost-plus contract.

There Is More

For additional tactics for negotiating the price, see Chapters 5 and 7.

5. Negotiating the Financing

Don't stop negotiating when you have agreed on price. Financing can be every bit as important, since price and financing are interrelated. The effect of a lower price and higher finance costs can be identical to that of a higher price and lower financing costs. This chapter describes additional alternatives that can benefit you as well as solve the problems of adversaries.

Seller Financing

In tight-money markets, sellers realize they have to take an active part in the financing if they are to sell their property.

As a matter of fact, the best bargains are possible in a tight-money market. Because many buyers are not even looking, due to high interest rates, truly motivated sellers not only cut their prices but provide below-market seller financing as well. For seller financing, a loan must either be assumable, or the seller must be willing to refinance with an assumable loan and carry back a second mortgage.

105

In a seller's market, with more buyers than sellers, significant price discounts and/or seller financing will not be readily obtainable.

Subject to versus Loan Assumption

If there is an assumable loan on a property, you as buyer should consider purchasing the property subject to the loan rather than agreeing to a loan assumption. When you take subject to a loan, you realize there is a loan on the property, and if you wish to keep the property you have to make the loan payments. However, if you don't, you have no personal liability, as you never agreed to pay.

In a loan assumption you agree to take the property and assume the primary responsibility for the loan. If you fail to make payments, not only can you lose the property but you might be liable for a deficiency judgment, the difference between the amount of the loan and the price received for the property at a foreclosure sale.

In some cases, deficiency judgments are not possible. If they are not, then it makes no difference if you assume the loan or take subject to it. (Check with an attorney in your state.) When deficiency judgments are possible, a buyer should take subject to loans and a seller should encourage the buyer to assume the loan, as he would otherwise remain primarily liable.

Step Interest

When the seller is reluctant to provide financing, a step interest proposal is often irresistible, because it appeals to natural avarice. Step interest, simply stated, involves raising the interest rate each year or two. For example, a loan might be structured as follows:

9% Years 1–2
11% Years 3–4
13% Years 5–6
15% Years 7–8
17% Until paid (or balloon payment is due)

Your state usury laws should be considered, although seller financing is generally exempt from usury.

As a buyer, you would probably want to refinance as soon as the contract interest rate exceeded market interest.

Interest Is Too High

When a buyer objects to the interest rate on seller financing or a required new loan, there are several approaches to minimize the expense.

"If you could get eight percent financing, would you be satisfied?" The answer to this question will likely be positive. You could continue with, "Since interest is deductible from income taxes, if you were in a combined 33 percent tax bracket (for both state and federal income tax) then the 12 percent interest only costs you eight percent with Uncle Sam picking up the balance."

Another approach: "What are you currently getting in interest on your savings? You mean you're getting eight percent? Why, this interest is only four percent more than your savings interest. At four percent, I think it's a real bargain."

Moratorium on Payments and/or Interest

A full price offer with a loan assumption and seller carryback financing can be very attractive to a seller. A variation is an offer where the payments on the carryback loan do not start for a specified period of time, such as one year. The net effect of such an arrangement is that the buyer is more likely to have a positive cash flow. The buyer has a year to use that cash flow to improve the property, which could then produce greater income and a positive cash flow when payments begin. If the moratorium is just on payments, there is negative loan amortization, with more money owed at the end of the year then at the beginning. If the moratorium also applies to the interest, the buyer receives the equivalent of a significant price reduction.

A Texas lending institution recently accepted an offer for a 200-unit apartment complex where the purchaser paid 20 percent down and agreed to use all revenues received for property improvements and repairs. (This was insured by a separate property management contract.) The lender agreed to an interest and total payment moratorium of two years. This unique arrangement, while the equivalent of a major price discount, increased the lender's security and rid the lender of a large foreclosed property. The buyer in this instance agreed to personal liability on the loan.

If a purchaser wants a moratorium from you, be certain the down payment is sufficient, so that default is unlikely after the moratorium period. Also, require that the cash flow go into the property, not into the pocket of the purchaser, to discourage a later default. Try to give a moratorium only on payments, not on interest, as the effect of an interest moratorium is a substantial price reduction.

Down Payment

When a seller objects to a low down payment and you as a buyer know, from the type of loan (FHA or VA) and the period that the owners have had the property, that they probably purchased with an even lower down payment—a good argument is, "Mrs. Jones, when you purchased this home how much of a down payment did you make?" This will usually bring some hemming and hawing or even a "What difference does that make?" but it is nevertheless a very effective blow to the seller's position. You should continue with, "I am not very much different than you were at my stage of life. I have high hopes for the future and limited cash. Where would you be today if, when you purchased this home, the seller had demanded $_____ down payment?"

This argument does not consider the seller's needs, which can be separately addressed by: "Mrs. Jones, if you were to receive $_____ cash, I imagine you would place most of the money in a bank or savings and loan association. Isn't that correct? Do you know what interest they are paying today? It is eight percent on a one-year certificate of deposit? I am offering you ten percent interest, which is 25 percent more than the bank will give you, and it's fully secured by your home. It amounts to getting 25 percent more for your house. Instead of $100,000 it is like getting $125,000. Does $125,000 for your home interest you?" This argument is extremely effective to convince sellers who don't need the money to carry the paper. If, however, they want the cash to purchase another property, point out that financing with a similar low down payment is possible.

Seller Refinancing

When the seller wants a greater down payment because he needs the cash, suggest that he refinance the property with an assumable loan, which would likely be an adjustable-rate mortgage. The seller keeps the cash generated by the refinancing in addition to your down payment. The seller then carries back a relatively small second mortgage, with you assuming the first. The result: the seller almost cashes out, and you get the property with a relatively low down payment.

Because the seller might have personal liability on the new loan, he might insist on a credit report on the buyer.

Borrowing from the Agent

If a real estate agent is representing the seller, talk to the agent about making an offer to purchase, specifying that you as buyer will be responsible for the agent's commission if the agent agrees to accept the commission in the form of a note or other paper. You are not trying to cut the commission; you are instead agreeing to be responsible for it. The agent is likely to agree, as he or she realizes that, unless the property is highly saleable, you as buyer are in the power position. Your offer can now provide a lower-than-requested down payment, since the owner's need for cash for the agent's commission has been diminished.

Offering Paper for Down Payment

At times, sellers don't need cash but want a significant down payment to reduce the danger of default.

You can meet the needs of such sellers by manufacturing paper. If you own another property in which the equity equals the requested down payment, you can give a new second mortgage on that property as your down payment. The seller now has the security of the property being sold, on which he or she is carrying the financing, as well as another property. The seller has the security needed, and you have not expended cash.

Using Paper To Buy

When they don't need the money, sellers often agree to finance buyers at a rate of interest below the market rate. They are often hard on the price but more flexible on terms. As a buyer, you can turn this to your advantage. Offer to buy a property using well-secured mortgages bearing a below-market rate of interest. If you can demonstrate to the seller that the security is as good or better than the property being sold, you should be able to convince the seller to accept the trade. The beauty of such an offer is that the paper can usually be purchased for a substantial discount from market value. The net effect of such an arrangement can be a significant reduction in price.

Paper is often advertised for sale in local newspapers, and many loan brokers and real estate brokers know of good paper available at discounts.

Zero Coupon Bonds

Zero coupon bonds are bonds that pay their face value when due. They are sold at significant discounts, since they pay no interest. For example, a $1,000 bond due in 20 years can usually be purchased for under $200. While most sellers want cash or income, this is not always true of owners of raw land. Because of taxes, land-holding produces negative cash flow. Such landowners are often intrigued with zero coupon bonds because they guarantee appreciation in value, have no carrying costs and fit well within an estate plan. For example, assume that an owner wanted $500,000 for a parcel of land, and in negotiation came down to $450,000. An offer of $2 million in 20-year, zero coupon bonds from a well-rated utility company in exchange for the land might look very interesting to the owner. (Note: there could be some negative tax consequences for the owner.) The bonds could likely be purchased for less than $400,000, which would mean a significant price concession. The seller or his or her heirs would have $2 million in 20 years.

If you, as the seller, are offered zero coupon bonds you should fully understand what you are agreeing to. Contact a stock broker to find the cash value of the bonds, and check with your accountant to determine your tax liability. You should also consider the fact that, because of leveraged buyouts, which have led to excessive corporate debt, corporate bonds now bear increased risks. A number of once-excellent bonds are now considered high-risk investments.

Blanket Mortgages

When a seller wants to reduce risk of foreclosure, consider agreeing to a blanket mortgage that covers additional property you own. The seller now has the security not only in the property sold but in your equity in other properties. A blanket encumbrance can make even very low down payments seem attractive. Any such arrangement should provide for the release of the blanket encumbrance as to individual properties upon agreed payments.

Assume the Private Loans

If a property has previous seller loans against it, consider assuming them, if possible, regardless of their interest rates and/or your ability to obtain better financing because private lenders, more often than not, will agree to discount the loan. It is the unusual person who will not agree to at least a 10 percent discount on the loan, and it is not unusual to see sellers agree to discounts of 30 percent or even greater. The previous seller has been getting a payment each month, which likely gets spent, and the thought of a large lump sum usually is very tempting. The net effect to the buyer is, of course, a further price reduction. You should negotiate the reduction using the techniques described in Chapter 4.

Seller Financing Discount

Sellers will often hold tight on price but will agree to carryback financing. This can be used to your advantage. About a year after the sale, consider contacting the seller and saying that you have some excess funds. (Any earlier, you risk angering the seller.) Indicate you are willing to pay off the loan if the seller will agree to a reasonable discount. The temptation of cash is especially strong if the financing is largely seller profit. The seller won't view it as a price cut, which it is, but rather as taking less profit and getting it now. Investors who consistently use this technique say that the chances of at least a 10 percent reduction for a payoff are better than 50 percent, and in at least 25 percent of cases a 20 percent or greater reduction has been reported. This really gives the buyer another bite at the apple after the sale.

Sharing Appreciation

The idea of the seller participating in future appreciation of the property can be an almost irresistible lure to convince a seller not only to finance a buyer with a modest down payment but to give the buyer below-market financing as well. This financing can reduce the buyer's risk significantly and can lead to a positive cash flow. For example, assume a sale was structured with 10 percent down and the balance financed by the seller at nine percent interest. The terms might also state that any sale within 10 years requires the original seller's consent. After 10 years, the property is to be appraised and placed on the market. When it is sold, the original seller receives the loan balance plus 50 percent of the appreciation in value from the original sale price.

The benefits to the buyer are a very low down payment, income and tax benefits for 10 years and half of the appreciation. The seller also benefits from a sale where risk of default is reduced because of reasonable loan terms, interest income for 10 years and half of the appreciation in value. Presented as an alternative during negotiations, shared appreciation is the type of creative solution that can break a deadlock.

Subordination

Subordination, where an owner agrees to carryback financing that will be secondary to a later loan, is generally unethical conduct and is to be avoided. There are times, however, when subordination offers are reasonable and ethical for all parties.

When an owner has a number of lots for sale, immediate construction of quality structures on several of the lots will enhance the value of the other lots. An agreement to build within a stated period a home of a set number of square feet, in exchange for the owner agreeing to subordinate the purchase loan to a construction loan for an agreed amount, would be a reasonable proposal. As buyer, you could likely get a loan for the entire construction cost, since this will be a first mortgage on the land and structure. The construction lender would, therefore, have reasonable security. When the property is sold, the lot seller will be paid.

The procedure described here is ethical. Unethical use of subordination is covered in Chapter 8.

Buyer Credit

Any sale where you as a seller will be carrying part of the financing should be subject to your satisfaction with the buyer's credit report. Without this contingency, you would have to go through with the sale, even if you discovered that getting money from the buyer had been found by others to be tantamount to obtaining blood from a turnip.

Your Credit

Your offer calling for seller financing will be strengthened if you include with it a copy of your TRW credit report and/or financial statements.

Prepayment Penalty

Prepayment penalties are regulated by state law. If you include a prepayment penalty clause in seller carryback financing, make certain that it does not exceed any state limitations. Legal services should be sought.

If you will be paying off a below-market-rate loan because you are selling the property, it is suggested you tell the lender you will consider paying off the loan if the prepayment penalty is waived. A lender who knows you're selling will be negotiating from a position of power and will refuse to do so. But if the lender doesn't know of the sale, you will appear to be in the position of power, and the waiver will likely be agreed to in writing if you pay off the loan within a designated period of time.

Late Payment Penalties

Specifying late-payment penalties in any carryback financing reduces the likelihood of late-payment problems. Because many states have limitations on late-payment penalties, consider legal help in drafting the required clause.

Points

Points are a percentage of the loan. When a buyer obtains a new loan lenders require points be paid. Three points on a $100,000 loan would be $3,000. On FHA loans points are negotiable between buyer and seller; on VA loans they are paid by the seller (consider this if you accept an offer contingent on VA financing); normally, on conventional loans the buyer (borrower) pays. However, some buyers insert provisions in offer forms requiring the seller to pay a portion or all of the buyer points. Using computer desktop publishing, some buyers insert it into the boilerplate so it looks like a standard form and is likely to go undetected. The net effect is the seller receives several thousand dollars less, and the unethical buyer avoids several thousand dollars of loan costs.

Balloon Payment

A balloon payment is a final payment on a loan greater than the normal monthly payments. Such payments are common in seller-financed loans and in loans made by noninstitutional lenders such as loan brokers. Normally, a loan with a balloon payment has monthly payments based on a long-term amortized loan, but the loan is all due and payable at an early date (usually between three and ten years).

If the borrower cannot obtain new financing, the lender would have the right to foreclose, or the lender might write a new loan at a higher interest. While it is preferable for a buyer not to have a balloon payment, this is not always possible. As a buyer you want the time until any balloon payment is due to be long enough for sufficient appreciation to make refinancing relatively easy. As a seller, you want a fairly short period. When the loan has a balloon payment due in a short period of time, such a loan can be sold on the secondary mortgage market for less of a discount than one with a longer balloon payment period.

Due-On-Sale Clause

A due-on-sale clause requires a loan to be paid in full if the property is sold. This clause is enforceable. As a buyer, you prefer not to have a due-on-sale (alienation) clause in seller financing. The absence of such a clause allows the loan to be assumed, which could help you in selling the property. It could even mean a higher resale price if the assumable loan offers attractive financing.

Land Contracts

Before you buy or sell on land contract, be certain you understand the state laws on buyer's and seller's rights. Generally, land contracts have been easy to foreclose upon default. In some states the courts have made foreclosure more difficult than mortgage foreclosure. The result can be a nightmare to the seller.

Wraparound Loans

If there is an assumable below-market-rate loan on a property, a seller or seller's agent should seriously consider carryback financing and a wraparound or all-inclusive mortgage. A wraparound loan is one written for the amount of the underlying debt plus the amount of seller's equity being funded. For example, suppose the buyer has offered a price of $120,000 with $20,000 down. Assume also that the offer is based on assuming a $50,000, seven percent loan and you as seller carry back a second mortgage for $50,000 at 11 percent interest. As offered, you would receive 11 percent on your equity. However, if a wraparound loan were used and the seller were to pay you 11 percent on a $100,000 loan (written to cover the $50,000 first mortgage as well as your equity), you would receive not only 11 percent on your equity but a 4 percent override on the first mortgage, giving you a true 15 percent return.

$$\left.\begin{array}{l} \$50{,}000 \text{ first } 7\% \\ \$50{,}000 \text{ equity} \end{array}\right\} \ \$100{,}000 \text{ at } 11\%$$

A further advantage of a wraparound loan is that the seller immediately knows if payments are being made on the first mortgage, because he or she makes them.

The buyer will, of course, prefer to assume a below-market loan to take advantage of below-market financing. Before you agree to an assumption, consider the value of the below-market financing. It will be easier to get the buyer to agree to a wraparound loan at a reasonable rate of interest than to a price increase, although your net benefit with the wraparound loan could be greater.

Usury

Too good a deal for you could well turn out to be a bad deal. State law governs the maximum interest that can be charged in a transaction by parties not licensed as lenders. In some states, sellers who finance buyers are exempt from usury requirements. Depending on your state, a contract calling for an illegal rate of interest could result in any interest being uncollectable. If interest is paid, it might have to be returned with a penalty in some states. In other states, a low legal rate of interest will apply in cases of this type. Because you have a buyer willing to pay a set rate of interest doesn't mean you can collect it. Because a bank charges a certain rate doesn't mean you can charge the same rate. If there is any doubt in your mind, check with an attorney.

Compensating Balance

Lenders such as banks making short-term unsecured loans or loans secured by other than first mortgages on real property might require a compensating balance. The lender asks that you keep a minimum deposit in either a low-interest or no-interest account. The effect of a compensating balance is to increase the effective rate of interest you pay. For example, if you had a 12 percent loan but were required to keep on deposit an amount equal to 25 percent of the loan in a no-interest checking account, you have actually only received 75 percent of the loan proceeds but will be paying 12 percent on 100 percent of the proceeds. The net result is a 16 percent interest rate. Before you agree to a compensating balance, be certain you fully understand to what you are agreeing.

Shop the Lenders

Different lenders offer different types of loans and loan terms. Your individual needs will determine what loan is best for you. For example, if you intend to sell a property within a year or so, you want a loan with lower loan origination fees, even if the interest is slightly higher. If you intend to keep the property for a long period, you want to get as low an interest rate as possible, and you might be willing to pay additional loan origination fees to get the lower rate.

Besides shopping lenders for the best loan to meet your particular needs, consider that what the lender quotes is not cast in stone. Lenders' loan rates have an aura of legitimacy to them so that borrowers will seldom negotiate. Very often, rates will be lowered for larger down payments, and points might be lowered by opening an account with the lender.

Agents for mortgage companies often receive a percentage or all of the loan origination costs (points) above a particular limit. The loan representative will, therefore, quote points that will benefit the agent. Knowledge of this fact can benefit you, even though the agent has indicated he cannot go any lower. One borrower recently called a company where an agent had indicated a loan would cost two and a half points. He spoke to another representative in the same company and told him what had been quoted, but did not indicate it was from the same company, and asked if they could beat the costs. The result on a $200,000 loan was three-fourths of a point less—a $1,500 saving.

Negotiate with Lenders Early

Negotiate for loans well in advance. If you can't get a commitment in writing as to terms, consider going elsewhere.

Banks and savings institutions are not above unethical conduct. A tactic often used is to approve the loan, with costs and/or interests just a little higher than quoted, after delays and an imminent deadline. Out of desperation, you will be forced to accept. Tactics such as this point out the need to negotiate early. The less desperate you are to get a loan, the better the terms are likely to be.

Your Own Bank

Talk to several lenders before you contact your own bank or savings and loan. You can now say, "_____ offered me $_____ at __ percent" when the competition has offered a more attractive loan. You might mention that if you took the loan from the competition you would have to transfer your checking and savings accounts. Depending on the size of these accounts, this could be a strong incentive, especially for smaller banks.

Your Trust Account

If you have a significant trust account as a broker or attorney, make certain the lender understands you have a trust account on deposit with that lender. The lender will understand that your loan request should get special consideration, usually as to interest rate. Don't threaten to move the account or make demands.

While you cannot directly benefit from use of trust monies, the benefit in this case is indirect and is not to the detriment of others.

Stick with a Lender

The more you borrow from a lender, the greater your power with that lender. When you have a large number of loans with a lender your financial well-being is of great concern, giving you additional leverage when you want to recast a loan at lower payments or to apply for additional loans.

Financing Too Good To Be True

You might be offered nonowner financing way below market. The usual story is that the person represents foreign investors, usually Arab or Japanese, and they have several hundred million dollars they want to commit in quality U.S. loans. The figures quoted you will be significantly less than the market rate in your area. The loan representative might ask for a fee at the time of application. More likely, you will only be asked for a small processing charge; however, the contract you sign will obligate you to a fee of between two and six percent of the loan amount upon loan approval and/or lenders' money being paid to the disbursement bank. Your loan will be approved, and you will get many papers to sign and have notarized by the foreign banks. There will be technical delays in the payout caused by ambiguous forms improperly filled out, etc. What it all boils down to is you paid for a loan, as did others, and everyone will shortly disappear.

Tax Consequences

You should understand the tax consequences of your sale before negotiating, not after an agreement is reached. For example, the Tax Reform Act of 1986 made the advantages of installment sales unavailable to dealers. One dealer, unaware of the changes, made a land sale with $20,000 down and found a total state and federal tax liability of almost $80,000. To make matters worse, most of the $20,000 down went to pay a broker's commission.

6. Negotiating Other Issues

Price and financing are not the only issues for negotiation, and at times are not even the most important issues. Negotiation involves a complete agreement, and all terms must be agreed to.

"It's Not Negotiable"

During negotiations, your adversary might indicate that a particular point is not negotiable. Your reaction to this assertion should be, "Why?" When you understand the party's reasoning, you might find that only one aspect is nonnegotiable or that you can in fact negotiate.

Even when an issue is nonnegotiable, you can negotiate *with* it. That is, use your agreement as a bargaining chip to be exchanged for another benefit. For example, agree to hold the matter in abeyance even though the other party indicates it can't be bargained for. Then when you are having difficulty negotiating another point, use the first issue to gain your point without having to give any new consideration.

Everything Is Negotiable

If you give in on price, you can, in effect, get back all you have given by getting your adversary to agree to pay costs you would otherwise be obligated to pay. These could include escrow costs, abstract costs, title insurance, appraisal fees, loan origination fees and loan prepayment penalties.

Other ways to offset price are to: (1) lower interest rates on seller financing, (2) provide for no payments and/or interest on seller financing for a period of time (moratorium), (3) include personal property with the sale. The same bottom line can be arrived at by more than one means.

Insistence upon What You Don't Want

Assume you are negotiating a lease as a tenant. Consider asking for an option to purchase at a price to be determined by an appraisal. This is a good tactic when an owner does not want to sell. Table this matter until later and continue your negotiations.

By a reluctance to accede in matters you are willing to agree to, you create phantom issues that have all the appearances of real ones. You can use these as concessions, gaining something in return without actually giving anything. The other side feels they got what they wanted, and you have been able to substantially hold to the position you desired.

Seller Financing

When you don't need or want seller financing, ask for it at below-market interest. You can use it later as a bargaining chip for a significant price reduction. Using amortization tables, you can show the dollar value of the below-market financing.

In seller financing, as buyer you want to negotiate out prepayment penalties. You also want the loan to be assumable. Of course, as seller you would want the opposite.

With new financing, the question of who pays loan costs is negotiable. As buyer, try to get the seller to pay new loan costs, or at least share them.

Collection Accounts and Tax Services

If there is to be seller financing, a seller might want to set up a collection account. The seller should try to negotiate that the buyer pays for this account or splits the monthly fees.

Tax services let an owner know if property tax is being paid. Normally, there is one advance payment of around $50. As a seller, you want the buyer to pay this charge.

Blind Problem

At times, what you are negotiating is not the real issue. A questioning approach is useful here; it normally uncovers the problem. For example, a tenant might complain about maintenance when the real problem is another aspect of the lease. It could be a secret agenda to negotiate an option to purchase.

Open Issue

If there is one area that cannot be resolved, consider calling it an open issue and continuing with all other areas of contention. The open issue can generally be resolved as part of a package agreement.

Contingencies

As a buyer, consider making your offer contingent upon the approval of leases, contracts and restrictive covenants. You might also want the offer contingent upon a final mechanical, electrical, plumbing and structural inspection, with the seller either making needed corrections before closing or refunding your deposit.

If there is any danger of not obtaining financing, consider a financing contingency clause. Be specific about the dollar amount of the loan, interest rates and loan costs. They should be above current rates, so a slight change in rates does not affect the agreement, but you gain protection against a major change.

Other contingencies to consider include sale of another property or approval of all leases. An offer contingent upon an appraisal showing a set value gives you the basis for renegotiating price if the appraisal is low.

Keep in mind that you may waive contingencies in an agreement for your benefit. Also keep in mind that the more contingencies an offer contains, the less likely the offer will be accepted.

Lease Terms

As a tenant, you want the greatest flexibility possible. You would probably be better off with a fairly short-term lease with a number of renewal options that give you the benefits of a long-term lease but none of the restrictions. You want to eliminate or keep at a minimum rental security deposits such as property "damage bonds" and the last month's rent. If you must pay them, try to negotiate that they be placed in an interest-bearing account with the interest credited to you.

As a lessor, you want as large a security deposit as possible, consistent with your state laws. You probably want to call deposits damage bonds because you would pay no tax on them unless they were forfeited. If you collected the last month's rent in advance, it would be taxed as income in the year received. You will want the tenant to agree to hold you harmless for any injury to another caused by the condition of the premises and to indemnify you for any loss you suffer. You also want the tenant to carry high-limit liability insurance that protects both you and your tenant. Check commercial lease form books and property management manuals as to types of leases and additional clauses.

Your success in negotiating lease terms depends a great deal upon your power, both real and perceived.

Consumer Price Index

If you are giving a long-term lease or an option to purchase that will extend for a long period, you want to receive the value negotiated. Because of inflation, dollars received in the future could have less of purchasing power than when the agreement was entered into. To solve this problem, consider tying the lease or option to the Consumer Price Index or some other inflation index. You thus lock in the purchasing power of future rent or purchase payments.

As a buyer or tenant, you want to base the inflation factor on a percentage of the Consumer Price Index. An argument to use is that the index includes interest fluctuation on housing costs. Since the owner probably has locked in his or her housing costs with a mortgage and has little other debt, the Consumer Price Index is not a true measure of the effect of inflation on the owner. Many leases are negotiated with a factor that is 50 to 70 percent of the Consumer Price Index, rather than 100 percent.

Tie Leases to the Loan

If you have an underlying adjustable-rate mortgage, you don't want a tenant on a long-term fixed rental. Otherwise, increased interest rates could result in negative cash flow. Consider tying in leases to the index used for your adjustable loan.

Tenants

If you are buying a property currently occupied by tenants and you wish to use the property for yourself or another tenant, try to require, as a condition for closing, that the property be vacated. Make the seller either evict, give notice to, or pay the tenants.

Business Opportunity Sales

In sales of businesses, a number of special items must be negotiated. Examples are the valuation of the stock in trade, price for accounts receivable and special contingencies such as transferability of lease and licenses.

Inventory can be evaluated at cost or based on present wholesale prices. In a period of rising prices, a seller wants prices based on present prices, while a buyer wants prices based on prices actually paid. If some of the inventory is shopworn, the buyer wants to negotiate a price based on a percentage of cost, say, 85 percent. A seller wants 100 percent, or as close to it as possible.

Standard Forms

Just because a form is printed does not mean it is a standard form, even if it says so. With a computer and a laser printer, anyone can print forms. When a form appears to be standard, people assume everything is all right. A form adds an aura of legitimacy to an agreement. People will argue over what goes in the blanks but not over the form itself.

Review all forms. Everything is negotiable, including all preprinted clauses.

If you have a number of tenants, have a standard form printed up for the leases. When lease terms are printed they take on an air of legitimacy, and tenants are less likely to object to a form than to typed proposals.

The fact that all other tenants have agreed to the clauses also has a strong effect on getting tenants to agree, even though the agreement of others has no bearing on the reasonableness of the clauses

Titles, Surveys, Etc.

If there is a minor title problem or if a survey reveals a problem, a seller should negotiate a clause giving him the right and a stated time period to rectify the problem before the buyer is released.

Personal Property

When personal property is included, it should be listed either in the purchase contract or in an addendum.

After the total price is agreed upon for the property, you, as buyer should negotiate the amount applying to real estate and the amount applying to personal property. You might want to check with your accountant beforehand. A higher valuation for personal property used with income property could offer tax advantages for depreciation. When real estate is reassessed for tax purposes upon sale, a lower price paid for the real estate could be advantageous. Be cautious, don't exceed the limits of reason.

Give Away the Building

Assume you have a large structure that has been vacant for a long time. Assume also you have no real equity in the structure, based on its present value and the loans against the property.

A technique in dealing with an economically strong prospective tenant is to offer a long-term lease at a market rent to assure you a positive cash flow, and to make the tenant a limited partner by giving him or her half the building. A giveaway such as this makes the property more valuable, based on a lease, so your equity actually increases, you have a positive rather than a negative cash flow, and you have a tenant who will stay. Your tenant gets back part of the rent in profit, and really a lot more, because the rent is paying off the loan. The tenant also benefits from appreciation of the property.

Giving things away can therefore be very profitable for both sides. The beauty of this tactic is, if the prospective tenant can use the space, it becomes an offer he or she just can't refuse.

Equity Position

If you are negotiating for space and the lessor is in desperate financial condition, you have the power to ask for—and get—access to the lessor's books. Rent that gives the lessor a break-even cash flow and renewal options could be negotiated even though what you're offering is a below-market rent, because the alternative could be loss of the property in foreclosure.

Besides minimum rent, you could also negotiate an equity position in the structure as a limited partner without a separate capital contribution. IBM and AT&T have both asked for and received equity positions based on their power. Lenders on shopping centers and office buildings have also negotiated an equity share. They realize that they are in a power position in a tight-money market, and money can bring more than just interest. All they have to do is demand it, and borrowers eventually will come around.

Give Them the Name

To many people, prestige is extremely important. In a lease for a significant portion of a commercial structure, a lessor has a significant noneconomic bargaining chip, the name of the building. For example, if your tenant is Harmon Industries, the name Harmon Plaza could be effective. The dollar difference could suddenly fade into insignificance.

An effective way to present this is to take an artist's rendering and superimpose the proposed name of the structure. Don't underestimate the value of the name in bargaining. Having the owner's name on the building does not bring in dollars, but a tenant's name will get you the lease and keep the tenant there.

Keep the Name

If a building has a family name on it and it is for sale by a family member, a concession to consider is an agreement to keep the family name on it. It might seem minor to you, but to the seller it could be a significant concession.

If it is an office building, think carefully about giving this concession, as it could be useful in the renting of the property.

The Commission

Many owners resent very much paying what they feel is an obscene commission for what they consider very little effort. This attitude can be used against owners. Your agreeing to pay the $7,000 real estate commission will often leave the seller ecstatic although he might have also agreed to cut the price $35,000. You are taking advantage of the inability to see the forest for the trees syndrome, which affects owners when it comes to paying broker fees.

Warranties

Under state law there may be implied warranties that structures have been built according to codes. The law in your state may also require disclosure of any known defects. Express warranties go beyond what is known; they are promises by the seller as to the condition of the structure. A statement that "All electrical, mechanical and plumbing systems and appliances are in good and proper working order" is a warranty, and the seller could be liable if it can be shown that this was not the case at the time of the sale. As a buyer, negotiate for warranties, but as a seller, consider them dangerous. If you are the seller, it would be far better for the purchase agreement to provide for an inspection by the purchaser and then allow you to correct any defect discovered or to return the buyer's deposit

In one case where the seller warranted condition, it was discovered after the sale that the fire suppression system did not meet current standards. The cost to correct it was over half the sale price, and the seller was held liable. While this is a horror case, think twice before you warrant anything.

It is possible to obtain private insurance on the physical condition of homes. Home protection plan coverage customarily includes the roof, appliances and major systems. The form of coverage and who pays for it is, of course, an item for negotiation.

If a seller makes a representation that you believe is false or have doubts about, you should ask, "Are you willing to include that representation as part of any agreements?" If he says yes, you have a warranty that could be valuable; if not, he will have retreated and will be placed on the defensive—so you will have gained power.

Satisfaction

Don't agree, as seller, to do work to the satisfaction of the buyer; you may be dealing with the one person who is never satisfied. Agreeing to do such work is an invitation to a lawsuit. Rather than agreeing to do any work, you would likely be ahead if you adjusted the price instead.

Use Their Impatience

In a situation such as a lease extension, when there is little danger of your adversary going elsewhere, one way to treat a request you are not interested in accepting is to say, "Let me get back to you on Tuesday." Don't call on Tuesday. Wait until at least Friday to say no. If the tenant calls you before then, it means he or she is quite anxious and you are dealing from a position of power.

Slip in the Biggie

Toward the end of lease negotiations, a tactic used by some lessors and leasees is to ask for a series of minor concessions and clauses likely to be agreed to after the basic rental has been set. After a number of these very minor items, one that really isn't so minor is suggested. With the string of approvals, the biggie is likely to slip through.

Make Them Compete

When you are not getting concessions you feel you must have, and have previously mentioned another property, what is apparently an exit statement can become a catalyst for concessions: "I would like to thank you for meeting with us here today. I want to be honest with you. What you're able to [pay or sell at] is not in our best interests. I'll probably commence negotiations on _____ within the next few days. You should be able to [buy or sell] a property at your $_____ price if you wait long enough. I wish you all the luck in the world, and perhaps we can get together in the future." The chance of losing you as a buyer or seller is a motivation. Your adversaries may not like your deal, but they also don't want someone else to get it. It could set you back at the table.

Bluff the Agent

If there are agents involved, sellers often take the position that, since they are taking less (less than what often was a price based more on optimism than reality), the agent should also take less. They will often indicate that unless the agent agrees they will not accept. Agents often cave in to this demand, but it is usually a bluff. The owner wants to sell and has agreed to pay a percentage of the sale price. Now that there is a deal, the owner is really attempting to rewrite the agreement.

As an agent, you should not cave in. The power is really in your hands. The more the seller thinks you need the money, the less he will offer to pay you.

When They Ask for Something More

Be prepared for the opponent who asks for something additional after you thought you had completed the negotiation. The way to handle this is to respond either:

1. "I am glad you brought that up because I realize I neglected to mention [something you wanted that outweighs what the opponent is asking for],"

or

2. "I don't see any problem. We'll just [adjust price or make another change at least as desirable as what you are giving]."

The result is you're not just taking a weak defensive position for some minor point; you are on a power offensive.

7. Impasse

Impasse is a deadlock, a situation where concessions have ceased without agreement. Neither party is able or willing to make a further concession.

While it is possible one or both parties have reached a point where no further concessions are economically possible, more likely one or both parties are holding out in the belief their adversary will give in to their demands.

Greed

Trying for the last possible dollar or a win-lose situation, where you humble your opposition, usually results in impasse. People who want to be big winners want the other side to be big losers. They tend to make few deals. Their power is seldom sufficient to make their opposition roll over and play dead. If this is your goal in negotiations, you should expect very few successes and a great many people who will hate your guts.

Threats

A threat is a formula for a walkout or impasse. A threat turns a negotiation away from economics toward personalities. People will give in to demands during negotiation when the final agreement is still beneficial to them, but when a threat is made they tend to toughen up and deal largely from emotion. They then make decisions not necessarily in their best economic interests. Should you, in the heat of negotiations, threaten your opponent with personal or economic repercussions, apologize immediately, explaining that your rhetoric moved in advance of your brain. You should then ask for a short break and follow it with a minor concession if you hope for an agreement, not impasse.

Emotion

It is difficult dealing with a person who is ruled more by emotion than economics. Sometimes emotion makes any agreement impossible. Even though you try to make such a person see the benefits, sometimes neither you nor anyone else can convince him or her. For example, a developer was about to be foreclosed on a multimillion dollar project, in which he had taken great pride. One day before the expiration of his right to redeem from foreclosure, he received an offer that would have taken over the project and left him with a little over $100,000 in cash. He refused, saying he would rather see the lender take it away than give the property away for peanuts to a vulture. All decisions are not made from economic best interests.

When To Hold

It isn't easy to say no consistently under pressure. To hold a position requires a healthy self-image, but there are times when you should be firm.

It takes courage to risk losing a buyer, seller, lessor or lessee. In negotiations you need courage, but your courage should be based on the likelihood of success, not blind risk. Your perception of your power will affect your position. If you feel strongly that the other party will meet your position because to do otherwise would be against their best interest, then you should hold relatively firm. Similarly, if other renters or buyers want to meet with you, your position will be enhanced. A problem arises when the other parties' perception of your power is different. They might believe they are in the driver's seat with other available properties, buyers or renters that are equally desirable. Even when they have nothing else and need you or your property, they might try to bluff you into believing otherwise, which would weaken your position. In this case, it becomes a game of poker. Are they holding the cards, or are they bluffing?

Where Winning Is Losing

Holding out for an agreement on your terms is meaningless if the agreement is unlikely to be honored. In other words, taking an intransigent position in the hopes you will get a bargain may not be a bargain at all. Examples: so high a rent that a tenant defaults, a construction contract where the contractor goes bankrupt with a half-finished building, or a sale where the purchaser cannot make the payments to you.

Analyze Your Position

When you have reached a deadlock, analyze your position. A risk-benefit analysis will help put issues into perspective. Consider the benefits of agreement and the risks of failure to reach agreement. Worst-case scenarios would be either: (1) no agreement or (2) fully meeting your opponent's demands.

Ask yourself:

1. How badly do I want agreement?

2. What will happen if an agreement is not reached with this party or for this property?
3. What alternatives might influence my adversary?

Consider your financial strengths and your willingness to take risks in deciding your course of action.

If you can't take losing the deal, consider a concession. If you also can't fully meet the other party's demands and remain solvent, then you need an agreement—but not the agreement offered.

If you are dealing from real strength and don't really need reaching agreement, consider trying to show the other party your strength and then offer a minor concession so he or she can save face.

To paraphrase the words of a popular song, "You got to know when to hold and know when to fold."

Egos

Often negotiations fail because of egos, not because what is possible is not acceptable. When a person has continued to repeat a position it becomes very difficult for that person to back down from the position; it becomes a matter of principle rather than an evaluation of the merits of reaching an agreement.

Don't take an adjustment in position as a personal defeat. While you may want to convince your opponent you won't give an inch, you don't want to convince yourself that this is your position. It is hard to do, but don't let your decisions be ruled by your ego. If a deal is favorable to you, don't lose it because the other side refuses to give in at all. You can save face by asking questions of the other party and admitting the logic of his or her position.

In the same manner, your refusal to give in could be the cause of the deadlock. You can break the deadlock by giving a concession, which does not necessarily mean you meet the position of the other party. By giving *something* you allow the other party to save face and retreat from a position he or she is locked into.

As a Technique

Some people use impasse as a negotiation technique. They hold tight to a position, getting further and further concessions until the other party will concede no further. They then make a concession. Since people don't like to fail, concession is usually met with an agreement.

Time Limits

Setting a time when you must leave (to catch a plane, for example) reduces the chance of deadlock. As the time nears, parties tend to get more reasonable. To serve you, the time limit must not appear arbitrary ("I must reach an agreement by Wednesday or I will. . ."). A statement such as "Our first ads on the property will be in the Sunday Times" *really* sets a time limit, which can result in a desire to break the deadlock.

The Clock and the Calendar

When there is an impasse or a danger of one, the likelihood of agreement is enhanced by scheduling a negotiation session on Friday afternoon. Many people have things planned for Friday evening and the weekend, and the thought of working late Friday night or, worse yet, over the weekend affects them. A minor concession between 3:00 and 5:00 p.m. will often be greeted with open arms.

After people have put in time, especially on a Friday afternoon, they want an agreement. Otherwise their effort will be lost. Use the clock and the calendar as negotiation tools.

Set It Aside

When the other side brings up a problem that you really can't solve, a good approach is to say, "Let me make a note of that, and let's get back to it later." It could be simply a phantom issue raised for its negotiation effect. If your adversary does not raise it again, it was likely just that.

If there are a number of issues to be negotiated such as clauses in a commercial lease, the issues on which the two sides are deadlocked should be set aside until all other matters are resolved. This will increase the desire of the parties to reach an agreement when you finally get back to the matter. You might have several matters that must be set aside.

A Break

When it appears that there is a deadlock, it is a good time for a break. This time can be used to rethink your position and consider alternative tactics.

You can also use a break to develop informal relations with the other party. Discuss something the other party is interested in. When the other party likes you personally, it becomes difficult for this person to take and hold a strong position against you. Informal discussions can also be used to lead into a solution. A great many deadlocks have been broken in a washroom. The informal atmosphere is conducive to a "let's get this thing resolved" approach.

When either party starts getting personal or hostile, disputes have little chance of being resolved. A good approach is to allow things to cool off by saying,

> *"I think we are both letting our emotions take over, and you and I know this won't lead us to a solution. Let's take a break, say, of 20 minutes and have some coffee."*

Never adjourn a meeting, but "recess until tomorrow." An adjournment carries the image of an end; a recess implies continuation.

Change Environment

An impasse can often be overcome by a simple change in environment. Suggest another visit to the property if you are the buyer or lessee. You can use this visit to question and to find problems. The intent, of course, is to reduce your opponent's perception of his or her power.

Sometimes suggesting coffee or lunch is a good idea. A neutral location and a different environment does change attitudes. When you take a person away from his or her desk and his or her office, that person's perception of his or her power also will change.

Team Change

With a negotiating team of two or more members, the good guy–bad guy technique can be used to break an impasse. One member of the team has consistently seemed more reasonable than the other, who has been a tough negotiator. After impasse, the good guy and the bad guy argue over position, and the bad guy leaves. The adversary will have developed empathy for the good guy, who will want to reach an agreement quickly before that S.O.B. returns. This is a simple variation of the good cop–bad cop technique used by the police. When the technique is used against you, the other side wants an agreement and will make concessions to get one.

Change the Team Seating

When there is a deadlock, a good technique after a break is to change the seating. Interspace your members next to other parties, not opposite them. The effect is that the opponents tend to lose the feeling of drawing support from the members of their team.

If teams are at an impasse, try meeting one to one with the other team leader without the rest of the team. This approach is often conducive to an agreement because parties are no longer negotiating to impress members of their team.

Open Analysis

A verbal analysis, when put forth in a fair manner, can motivate parties to reach an agreement. For example, suppose you are negotiating with a tenant for a lease renewal.

> *"Let us analyze what will happen if we can't reach an agreement: (1) I will be out a tenant and probably a month's rent till I rerent the premises. (2) I'll have the cost to rerent as well as possible redecorating expenses.*

> *If you leave you will have (1) time and expense to find another location that may or may not be as desirable as this location and may or may not be as economical; (2) the direct moving expenses; (3) possible costs to modify the new space for your needs; (4) costs for a new phone system, stationery, signs; (5) costs to notify people you do business with as well as inconvenience to them. Now, what can we do to reach an agreement?"*

Review the Agreement

If you have agreed on a number of points, review them in order to minimize the difference.

> *"Let us review where we are as to points of agreement. You have indicated you wish me to leave (personal property) with the property and I have indicated that doing so is acceptable to me.*

> *"You want a June 1 closing date, and I have agreed to this.*

> *"You wanted me to carry back a second mortgage for around $50,000 at 10 percent interest all due and payable in seven years. I have agreed to this. Am I correct as to our agreements?*
>
> *"Now, you initially offered $150,000 for the property, and I had advertised it for $200,000. You have raised your initial offer to $170,000 and I have reduced my price to $184,000. Right now we are $14,000 apart, or a seven percent difference based on the original price. Do you want to lose your home for just seven percent?"*

You want to maximize the areas of agreement and minimize areas of disagreement; and by showing the disagreement dollars as a percentage of the original price, you make the disagreement seem minor. Consider suggesting that you work together to resolve the problem. If the other party agrees, it means you are both willing to compromise.

Participative Solution

Ask the other side for help when impasse is reached.

> *"How would you suggest we solve. . .?"*
>
> *"Is there any other area of the agreement that could be modified to allow. . .?"*

The more actively you can get the other party to seek a solution, the greater the likelihood of one being found and agreed to. The participative solution works especially well in the informal atmosphere of a recess.

> *"How can we reach agreement?"*
>
> *"Off the record, what is it going to take to reach a realistic agreement so I can go home?"*

Explain It Some More

In a deadlock, use a question technique to get the other side to modify their position.

> *"I understand what you are asking, but I really can't justify it from what you have said. Perhaps I don't fully understand your reasoning. Would you go through it once again?"*

> *"The facts that I have presented as to comparable values don't seem to justify your price. Perhaps I am missing something. Why are they so far apart?"*

The other parties are being asked to explain what may well be unexplainable. They will feel their power eroding against a factual assault, where they are asked to justify a position. You are playing the role of a reasonable person wanting to understand.

Alternatives

When a deadlock exists, bring out any alternatives you had considered in your planning strategy. Lease options, seller financing versus cash, percentage lease, deferred payments, etc., all open the discussion to apparent routes that can reach the same end.

Components

When you have an impossible problem, try to break it into the smallest components possible and discover the exact problem areas. Once you fully understand the problem, it can often be negotiated. For example, assume that the problem is price. As a buyer, you might consider offering a lower down payment with some carryback financing rather than the cash offer that had been refused. When we know precisely what we disagree on and where we have room to negotiate, we can often structure proposals that have a greater likelihood of becoming contracts.

Concessions

To break a deadlock, concessions are necessary. One or both parties must give in. If both parties hold their ground, neither can benefit. Negotiations at times resemble a game of chicken, with both cars running at each other. One must try to avoid collision, or they both suffer. The concession often doesn't have to be major, and it doesn't have to be in money; it can be in terms or simply changing a clause. You can use new information you discover during negotiation as basis for a concession: "That changes the picture if that's the case then...."

Be Reasonable

It is easier for people to give in to your position if you appear reasonable rather than arbitrary. Let them know you have considered their arguments and benefits in arriving at your position. "If it were not for _____ I would have offered only $_____."

Closeness

When you are physically apart, coming closer has the effect of confidentiality for a final offer, which should be conveyed in a lower voice tone. Be careful not to come too close, as invading another's space can be threatening. About three feet away is fine (two feet is too close).

Not Just for Agreement's Sake

You must ask yourself before every concession, "What will happen if no agreement is reached?" Don't continue to negotiate if you don't really care whether you get the deal at what you are offering. An agreement should not be for the sake of reaching an agreement; it should be for the benefits to be derived from the agreement.

Make Decisions Easy

Instead of a further price adjustment you could consider the following:

> *"We are very close, and I think reaching an agreement would be mutually beneficial. Even though I firmly believe that with my offer of $_____ I may have gone too far, nevertheless in the interest of the relationship I hope will develop between us, I am willing to pay all escrow and closing costs [title costs, etc.] if we can reach an agreement now. Isn't that more than fair to you?"*

In actuality, the costs might be far less than the price concession that would otherwise be necessary for agreement. Keep in mind that, if you would have otherwise split these costs, you're only giving half the costs involved.

A Turnaround

A tactic to use when dealing with a deadlock is to meet the particular demand but take back or modify any other element of the contract that has already been agreed to. Your chance of success will be based on how the other party views the concession you are asking in return.

The Switch and Assumption

A tactic often used by company executives is to sit back and watch the negotiation and not reveal their position in the firm. When the negotiation gets close but has reached impasse, that person says, "All right, you seem to be having some difficulty. I'll take over now." By using an assertive manner he or she takes for granted that his or her proposal, which includes a concession, will be accepted, orders one of his people to write it up and then starts thanking the opposition.

While an assumption of agreement will not ordinarily work, it will when handled with a switch after an impasse if done in an assertive manner.

Hypothetical Approach

By using a "what if?" approach you can explore the effect of concessions without formally making them, although both parties realize it is really an offer and not the hypothetical question it appears to be.

The hypothetical approach is an excellent way to break a deadlock. Parties are willing to make hypothetical concessions, thinking they can later retreat if the concessions are not met with reciprocity. In actuality, once made they have revealed a position and have set a new benchmark from which to negotiate.

Put Yourself in My Shoes

This argument is quite effective. For example, you could state,

> *"Put yourself in my shoes; now these are the facts. I know you wouldn't accept this offer if you were me. Therefore, let's try to reach an agreement. Why don't you raise your offer to $_____?"*

Note, you haven't said you will accept this offer, but that is what is being implied.

Make the Solution Their Solution

From your questioning you might believe you have a solution to the impasse. If you can make the solution appear to be your opponent's solution, you have turned a possibility into a probability. You can often lead in using the "if" approach. Then you say,

"Let me get this straight. From what you have said before and what you have just conveyed, you would consider a solution that involved _____. Am I correct?"

If you get a positive response, you accept and have an agreement.

Split the Difference

Deadlock practically cries out for the split-the-difference approach. There is no logic to it, and it isn't necessarily fair; but from small children we have accepted the premise there is nothing more fair than splitting the difference. It is hard for a person to appear fair and refuse to split the difference. It works far more often than it fails when there's a deadlock.

Empty the Pockets

An impasse breaker that also tends to be a tension breaker is to take out your wallet and count all the cash you have with you, then empty your pockets and take out all of your change. Do this without comment. Now state, "I can increase the pot by $_____." Add that figure to your last offer and state the total offer, pushing your cash across the table at your adversary. Such a tactic generally conveys that you have reached your limit. Often the adversary will laugh and accept your offer. He will then delight in telling friends how he took everything but your drawers.

One successful practitioner of this tactic offers to throw in her wedding band, providing the adversary will also take her husband.

Flip a Coin

Many people are gamblers at heart. When you are willing to meet the other person's terms if absolutely necessary to break the deadlock, you can often get the equivalent of a 50/50 chance of

the other party meeting your offer by simply pulling out a coin
and saying,

> *"We have an impasse. I have gone as far as I can, and you
> apparently have gone as far as you can. Nevertheless, I am
> willing to trust to the gods of chance. [Flip a coin and cover
> it.] Heads or tails? If you call it right, we have an agreement
> on your terms of $_____. If you are wrong, we have an
> agreement at my offer of $_____. You can call it, or, if you
> wish, you flip and I'll call."*

A great many people can't resist the fairness, and it appeals to
their risk instincts. While this is an unprofessional way to reach
agreement, it works. As a precaution, be certain to spell out the
agreement in clear terms before the flip, and immediately there-
after put it in writing.

Fair Value

When you present an offer that by its very nature appears fair, it
is difficult for the other side to say no. You should therefore consider saying,

> *"I am willing to pay fair market value [or sell at fair market
> value]. I am certain you don't want anything more than a
> fair price. Am I correct? Our problem is we disagree as to
> what is fair. I believe I have a solution. Let's agree on some-
> one to appraise the property. If the appraiser's value is closer to
> the value I have set, you pay the appraisal fee. If the appraisal
> is closer to the value you've set, then I pay the appraisal fee.
> Does this sound fair? Now, the appraisal value will be used for
> information only. It should be understood neither of us will be
> bound by it, but hopefully we will use it to negotiate a mutu-
> ally beneficial agreement. What I propose is that we make a
> list of the appraisers in the phone book with an MAI (or
> SREA) designation. We then either draw one name from a*

*lot or take turns eliminating appraisers until only one name is
left. Which method would you prefer?''*

The beauty of this approach is its absolute fairness, giving neither
side an advantage that will make an objecting party seem unfair
or arbitrary. While the agreement is that the appraisal will only
be advisory in nature and not binding, it will nevertheless be difficult for a party to refuse without loss of face an offer based on
the appraisal. As a variation you could say, "If you like, I am willing to accept the appraiser's figures as our agreement with the
limitation that I won't pay more than your figure or less than my
figure. Does this seem fair to you?" Before you hire the appraiser, put this agreement in writing.

Mediation

Mediation is the use of a neutral go-between to work with the
parties to reach an agreement. Unlike an arbitrator, a mediator fa-
cilitates an agreement. (An arbitrator makes the agreement.) Because a mediator cannot force parties to do what is against their
interests, mediation as a solution to an impasse is seldom ob-
jected to.

A mediator can frequently get parties to open up to him or
her as to their needs and desires. When parties meet in good faith
with a mediator, the chances of their agreeing to solutions rec-
ommended by the mediator are far greater than if they negotiated by themselves.

Take It or Leave It

When you are prepared to walk out, set forth your position as a
take-it-or-leave-it proposition, making it clear you have reached
your limit. This approach can also be used when you are negotiating from a position of power. The danger is that the other party
may think you really mean it when you don't. For example, a
large and prosperous property management firm was recently

placed on the market by a widow who had no experience in the business. She offered the firm to a major competitor who believed they were the only logical purchaser for the business. They gave her a take-it-or-leave-it cash offer at far less than the value indicated by a professional business appraisal she had commissioned. Three of her employees who had learned of the negotiations then made a cash offer of almost twice the amount proposed by the competitor. They did this through refinancing their homes and a loan from the bank where the firm conducted its business. After the sale, the competitor indicated to the widow they would have willingly paid more for the firm than the employees could have raised. Her response was, "You indicated you wouldn't negotiate. It was a take-it-or-leave-it offer, so we left it."

Walkout

Breaking off negotiations shows a firmness of purpose. Many negotiators use the walkout as a negotiation tactic. Be very careful if you have not reached your limit, because your adversary could believe you and go elsewhere.

On the positive side, if you walk out and the other party wants to sit down with you again, you know you are dealing from a position of power. If the party doesn't come back, then he or she has the power and you had better be prepared to make concessions.

If you threaten to walk, you had better walk—unless concessions are given. Threatening and then failing to do so destroys your credibility. It also indicates to the other party that he or she has the power.

After you have gathered your papers and put on your coat, if it appears the other party is not going to change positions, consider a little teaser to start up the process again. For example:

> *"You know, I have enjoyed working with you, even though we were unable to reach an agreement. You are really a strong negotiator. I really thought we could reach a mutually benefi-*

> *cial conclusion because* _____. *While I have some room left to negotiate, it is obvious to me* _____ *is your final position, and at that position agreement is not possible for us. Perhaps sometime in the future we will be able to work together where you have greater flexibility."*

Note, you have left on a good level. You have left room to negotiate, but the problem is that your opponent's position is still unacceptable to you. The result of this approach is frequently a concession while you are on your feet and a quick meeting of the minds. Walking out or threatening to walk out is brinksmanship negotiation. While risky, for some it has been a successful tool.

The Final Concession

Always save something for later—a final concession to use after deadlock to put an agreement together. The final concession must be large enough for the other parties to save face. Their holdout has been rewarded. They will be able to tell others how they bested you. There is, however, a delicate balance. Too great a concession, and they will feel it is just another concession with more on the way. It could encourage the other parties to hold their position.

To reduce the likelihood of the other party misreading your resolve, you could state, "If we can reach agreement right now, I'll _____. If we can't reach an agreement, I must withdraw this offer."

An interesting technique used by one negotiator for a final concession is, "This offer shall be good for exactly 10 minutes. If it is not acceptable to you, I apologize for wasting your time." The negotiator then sets an alarm watch, which she places on the table. When the buzzer goes off, she starts to put her papers together and leaves. The other party will often concede.

A variation of this approach is: "$_____ was the maximum [partner—principal, etc.] has authorized me to offer. However, I will take it upon myself to raise this to $_____. If you accept now,

I will personally stand behind the agreement. If not I will inform _____ that an agreement is not possible within the guidelines."

End of Session

When you terminate a negotiation session that has ended in impasse, try to strike as positive a note as possible. You want your adversary to think about how the impasse can be broken:

> *"Let's both do some thinking. I believe we should be able to come up with some creativity that will meet both of our needs."*

Consider handing your opponent an agreement, already filled out, which includes a minor concession.

> *"Here is the agreement I want; look it over. If you feel you must make changes, make them and initial them. Sign the agreement and send it back to me. If I can, I will sign it and we will have a deal. If not, we were unsuccessful."*

The result of this approach is likely to be a more realistic approach (concessions) in the counteroffer.

Reopen the Door

Time often works to resolve what was formerly unresolvable. Often a call several weeks or even months later about another matter, even a request for a charitable donation, can be used to revive negotiations. By simply asking as an afterthought whether your opponent purchased, sold or leased the property, you can determine if the need still exists. If needs have not been satisfied, you can put the ball back into play by pointing out it is too bad you were so far apart. Ask for a face-to-face meeting. Be prepared to make a concession. This would be a good time for a let's-split-the-difference approach.

8. Negotiation Dangers

Negotiations are not without dangers. There are dangers inherent in the process, as well as dangers with the people involved.

While negotiators should be tough, they also should deal with integrity. Unfortunately, some people place the end above the means and will embrace any tactic to reach the desired conclusion. To such negotiators, the first rule of negotiation has become, "There are no rules."

Besides dangers inherent in negotiations, we have included, with great reluctance, detailed warnings of what we consider unethical conduct. This material is not to be used as a blueprint for negotiations, but rather to recognize unethical conduct of others so you can protect your interests.

Your Misrepresentation

If you discover you made a misrepresentation, inform the other party of your error as soon as possible. It if was a material misrepresentation, follow up your verbal explanation with a written correction of the facts. You want to deal in real estate, not lawsuits.

If, after learning of your mistake, the other party continues to negotiate, he or she will have waived your misrepresentation.

Price versus Performance

Should a buyer want you to perform work, such as repairs, prior to closing, consider a price reduction in lieu of the work. Besides the possibility that the buyer will not be satisfied with the job, there is the danger it will end up costing you far more than envisioned. If the work is something you would not otherwise do, there is also the danger that you will do the work and the deal will not close for some other reason, leaving you out the cost of the work.

A good approach is to ask the buyers what they feel the work will cost. Because they want you to agree to do it, the buyers will normally quote a fairly low amount. An approach that smacks of fairness is now to say, "Because I would rather you handled it to see that it is done the way you want, I will reduce the price $_____" [add about 10 to 20 percent to the price quoted by the buyer]. This should cover any minor adjustments. "Does this sound fair to you?" To answer other than yes, the buyers will be saying they were unrealistic in the price estimate.

Termite Inspection

FHA, VA and some conventional lenders require a termite and structural inspection. The clauses in most purchase agreements require the seller to correct any damage or problems discovered. As a seller, you do not want to accept an offer that utilizes such language without modification. Never agree to do any work if the cost cannot be ascertained at the time of the agreement. Put a dollar limit on your obligations. If the inspection reveals a high cost, you then have the option of waiving your limit and proceeding with the repairs or of backing out of the sale

Deposit to Seller

While you want to show the seller the color of your money, you don't want the seller to get control of your deposit until after closing. If you give a deposit directly to a seller, there is the danger the seller will be unable to deliver clear title or the sale will fail for other reasons and the owner could be either unable or unwilling to return your deposit.

Deposits should go the neutral escrows, broker trust accounts or to attorneys' trust accounts, depending upon the type of closing.

Escrow for Seller's Work

If work is to be done by the seller after closing, as a buyer you want to make certain the work is completed (for example, a new structure where the parking area cannot be paved until the weather gets warmer). In this type of situation, withhold a sum of money sufficient not only to cover the work but actually more than sufficient to pay for it. In this way you can be assured it will be done. The money withheld should be placed in escrow, and, if the work is not completed by a set date, the amount should be forfeited to you as liquidated damages. Such a clause should be prepared by an attorney.

New Building Allowance

If you are selling a new structure that will be finished to a buyer's specifications, negotiate specific allowances for carpeting, tile, lighting fixtures, etc., based on retail prices at specified dealers and/or suppliers. This way you know your costs with a fair degree of accuracy.

You can also provide a definite dollar allowance for remodeling work for a new tenant.

Insurance Costs

In many areas, it is difficult to get adequate insurance coverage, or the costs can be excessive. What was formerly a minor expense can now be significant. Insurance costs for property with vacancies can be several times higher than those for occupied property.

If the building has a liquor store or bar, your liability might be tremendous. Several states have deep-pocket laws where building owners can be held liable for actions of drunk drivers when the bar was negligent. Because of these laws, the costs of insurance, when it is available for this type of building, have gone up significantly.

When negotiating a purchase of property other than a single-family dwelling, ask your insurance broker about availability of coverage and the cost.

Certify Costs

When owners have supplied operating statements or otherwise indicated costs, have the owner certify the completeness and accuracy of the material furnished. If the owner is reluctant, there could be problems. Keep in mind that operating costs seldom end up lower than figures given by sellers.

Audited Statement

For large properties, consider requesting an audited operating statement. Such a statement does not, however, guarantee accuracy, as auditors can be deceived.

Effect of Free Rent

In order to show an exceptional return, owners frequently offer incentives to tenants in the form of several months' free rent or gifts. With rental inducements, the scheduled rent could be unrealistically high and tenants are more likely to leave when their leases expire than in buildings where rental inducements were unnecessary. The result will be either an above-normal vacancy factor or the necessity to again offer rental inducements or reduced rent.

To protect yourself, insist on signed statements from the owner as part of the purchase agreement that inducements (either reduced rent or premiums of any form) were not used to rent the units. During escrow you should then check with tenants to verify what the owner has stated.

You should seriously consider having tenants sign a statement as to their rent, the lease period and any owner deposits held. As buyer, you are entitled to the deposit, because you are the one who will have to return it. Your closing statement must provide for these credits.

A worse-case scenario occurs when an owner has given several months' free rent to lease, but the free rent is at the end of the lease. Without checking with the tenants, you would not know of such an arrangement until well after closing.

Representative Unit

If the property you are negotiating is an older structure and you have only seen several of the units, make certain what you have seen is representative of the entire building. You might have been shown only exceptional or updated units. You want, as part of the purchase agreement, a statement that the seller warrants the units you have seen to be representative of the other units as well as the right to inspect every unit prior to closing.

Manager's Apartment

A common error on operating statements and brokers' pro forma statements is to show the rent applicable to the manager's apartment as being received. This is proper so long as providing of the apartment to the manager is shown as an expense. When this factor is forgotten, the expense figures are understated by the rent for one unit. In checking operating statements, be alert for this possibility.

The Lunch Negotiation

While several issues can be resolved in the nonthreatening atmosphere of a restaurant, complex negotiations can be handled better in a more formal setting. The danger is that issues will be left unresolved.

If the other party wants to meet for lunch, watch out for the alcohol. Three-martini negotiations can be disastrous, especially if your adversary is a professional (drinker, not negotiator).

Occupancy prior to Closing

Generally, it is not a good idea for a buyer to take possession prior to closing, even under a rental agreement. There is a good chance the buyer will find features or the absence of features he or she did not previously know of or consider, as well as faults both real and imagined. This can blow a sale apart.

If possession is given to a tenant prior to closing, it should be clearly on a month-to-month basis. The lease should provide for a significant rent increase after the first two months to encourage the tenant to leave if the sale falls apart. If you would let the buyer enter as a buyer in possession, you could not evict that buyer because he or she is not a tenant. There have been horror cases of a buyer in possession more than three years without making any payments while the parties fought in court over the contract.

Important People

People tend to react differently when dealing with well-known, important persons than with people who are closer to them in economic and/or social standing. Large defense contractors bring in well-known retired generals to complete negotiations against active-duty captains. The tactic works. A hard position is difficult to hold against someone you hold in awe. Charities often do the same thing, bringing celebrities into final real estate negotiations.

If you know why such an important person is being brought into the negotiations, you will be less likely to react in accordance with your adversary's plan.

Time for Closing

The quicker the closing, the less chance of problems arising. Difficulties seem to be in direct proportion to additional time taken for closing. Therefore, try to negotiate a closing as quickly as possible.

Look the Gift Horse in the Mouth

While most buyers and sellers in real estate are relatively honest, it seems the large dollar amounts involved serve as a magnet for thieves. Although you will occasionally come across a really exceptional deal, these are few and far between. You will find far more fantastic deals that *aren't* than *are.*

Be particularly alert when the other party claims urgency requiring an immediate decision. The odds are in your favor to reject such a situation. Unless you have completely checked out the situation and have had legal advice, beware the once-in-a-lifetime deals.

When To Worry

When the party you are dealing with lets you know how honest he or she is, your guard should go up. Seldom will an honest person feel it necessary to vouch for honesty, but it's difficult to find a dishonest person who doesn't let you know you're dealing with an honest person.

When people indicate they want to be completely honest with you, it is really an admission they haven't been completely honest with you in the past; and if the past is a blueprint for the future, don't expect perfect honesty now. When you are dealing with an "honest" person be especially alert and make certain any agreement has been reviewed by a real estate attorney before you sign. Don't let anything be left to a gentleman's verbal understanding, as you will find later the person was no gentleman and he will deny any understanding.

The Instant Friend

Beware of the party who takes an instant liking to you, issuing social invitations and/or picking up the check at expensive restaurants. Suddenly, you seem to have a brand-new best friend. Unfortunately, this best friend could have ulterior motives. What he or she may be out to do cannot be described in mixed company.

You should also be on your guard with the oversolicitous person who makes too much of a fuss over you. Get your snowshoes out, because this all too often is the prelude to a snow job.

The Superparent

When you are dealing with a much older person you might hear, "I don't have a family of my own. If I had a (son or daughter), I would have liked them to be like you. I would like to do something to help you; after all in my position a few dollars' difference is meaningless. Now here's what I propose. . . ."

Don't fall into the web of the superparent. This person is setting you up for a deal that can twist against you. Have any agreement the superparent prepares reviewed by a whole covey of attorneys

The Low Earnest Money Offer

Some purchasers will offer a relatively small earnest money deposit and a rather long period for closing. They usually have a reason for the low earnest money payment and long escrow—probably that they are selling another property for cash and closing isn't for 60 (or 90) days. The offer will include a provision that, in the event of buyer's default, your sole remedy as seller will be to keep the buyer's deposit. If you ask for details of the buyer's other sale, you can expect a vague response. What the buyer has really done is to obtain an option to buy, with the cost of the option being the earnest money. In a good market, you will be tying up your property for a long period for a buyer who will buy only if he or she obtains a buyer at a higher price before the closing. The only time you should consider such an offer is when you would look favorably on an option to buy under similar circumstances.

Keep in mind that the person putting in this offer is probably an expert, although of questionable ethics, and this expert thinks your property is worth more than the offer indicates.

As a general rule, the longer the escrow period, the bigger the deposit should be.

Deposits Other Than Cash

You might see an earnest money deposit in some form other than cash. A promissory note might be acceptable with a provision it would be payable in a matter of days, such as within five days of acceptance of the offer. In this way, you would not tie up the property for a lengthy period of time with paper that could prove to be worthless.

When a buyer offers a noncash security (such as gemstones with appraisals or trust deeds on other properties), as earnest money, be on your guard. While the noncash security might be only for security purposes and is not to be part of the purchase payment, the chances are great the security is next to worthless. The buyer is simply tying up your property without security. We have seen this tactic used a number of times but have never seen legitimate security offered.

Taking Different Paper

A number of sophisticated sellers have been defrauded by even more sophisticated, but dishonest buyers offering paper for real property. In one case, the buyer transferred almost worthless property (land without any possible access or available water) to an accomplice. The papers of sale showed the buyer had paid $1 million down and had given a first mortgage due in 12 months for $1 million to the seller. The seller then offered this $1 million dollar mortgage along with verifying appraisals to an unsuspecting party in exchange for free and clear property worth $1 million dollars. When the note was not paid, the defrauded seller discovered the land had been purchased for $12,000, and the person listed on the note had no assets. The buyer had mortgaged the property for over one-half million dollars and disappeared.

The above case points out the necessity for a seller's vigilance when taking a mortgage on anything other than the property sold. Don't rely on the buyer's appraisals. Unfortunately, there are too many "appraisers" who will sign anything for a price. Have your own appraisal made by someone with either an MAI or SREA designation. Also, make all parties provide you with their credit reports. Determine through your attorney if deficiencies judgments are possible in the event of borrower default.

Low-Ball versus High-Ball

Both these techniques are pure deceit and cannot be condoned by an ethical person. Be aware of them because they may be used with you as the victim.

The terms "low-balling" and "high-balling" come from the automobile sales industry. A low-ball figure is a sales figure below what you envisioned you would have to pay. It is given by a salesperson to get you excited about buying and to begin the actual negotiation process. If you have ever been low-balled by an auto dealer, you know that you sign a purchase agreement that goes to the sales manager for approval. Your salesman argues on your behalf (he or she is on your side, or seems to be). The salesperson comes back with the fact that it will take a little more. A question often asked is, "Can you pay $38 more a month?" Now the hard-ball selling begins. Low-balling was simply a process to get you to the table.

High-balling is just the opposite—a verbal quote given, subject to approval, for a trade-in or purchase from you. Again, the price is higher than you hoped, and it is simply a tool to get you to the negotiation table. Agents will often high-ball you with a prospective buyer who they know will pay $_____ for your property. It opens the door to them for a listing. After obtaining the listing, the unethical agent will then try to lower your expectations to prepare you for a low offer. While few agents practice tactics such as these, there are those who will treat you as fair game, with the end justifying the means.

Some lessees use a high-ball technique to get a lessor excited and then try to negotiate away with the small print what the big print gives. Similarly, the possibility of a bargain (low-balling) is often used to get people to the bargaining table.

If you feel you are being played with, tell the other parties you don't appreciate being high-balled or low-balled. They will know what it means. You have a right to be indignant. Ask if they want to give you their best price before you leave. Be prepared to leave.

In low-balling and high-balling, the price given appeals to the bargain and good dealmaker in all of us. We let our avarice rule us and get hoisted on our own petard. Protect yourself by learning to look the gift horse in the mouth.

Low-Ball Variation

A variation of the low-ball approach is often used by land salesmen selling either recreational or investment parcels, usually to unsophisticated buyers at inflated prices. The salesperson drives the prospective buyer to a remote sales office on the pretense that he or she has to get something. While there, the salesperson notices the price shown for the lot just looked at is about 30 percent more than the price he or she has quoted the prospect. The salesperson goes into another room, where the sales manager is, and asks about the discrepancy. The salesperson is told that there were several typographical errors in the sheet, that they were all corrected, and the salesperson should have received the changes. The salesperson explains that he or she quoted the old price, and the buyers want the lot. The salesperson finally persuades the sales manager to sell at the old price. However, it is understood that the salesperson will not get a commission. This whole conversation is staged for the prospective buyers in the next room who have heard every word. Now that the salesperson has worked so hard on their behalf and managed to get them such a bargain, they find it hard not to take advantage of this good fortune.

The Business Card Price

A variation of the high-ball tactic is practiced by a prospective buyer who gives you his or her business card. On the back, he or she writes a price, usually a fair price for your property. The person then tells you to contact him/her if you are interested in selling. When you do, the buyer wants to make a thorough inspection of the property and comes up with deductions from the price quoted. This person is usually a dealer who wants to buy for resale and has no intention of paying a fair price. The card price was merely the teaser.

Stupidity Ploy

Some sophisticated parties act stupid. They just don't understand your position and reasoning. They are irrational because of their obvious lack of understanding. The result is that you become frustrated. When you're frustrated, you are likely to make greater concessions than you would have if your adversaries understood your arguments. It's hard to argue with ''I don't understand," so dumbness ends up the winner. Beware. They may not be so stupid after all.

The Term-Changer

A good reason to be the one drafting the agreement is to avoid the term-changer, a person who makes minor changes in the contract to his/her own benefit, either contrary to or in addition to what was negotiated. This person gets his kicks by getting a little bit more, hoping it isn't enough to have you reject the agreement.

One way to avoid these tactics when your adversary prepares the document is to send a detailed letter setting forth your agreement to your adversary to "aid in drafting the contract." If your adversary still takes liberties in drafting, point them out and make the necessary changes, which you should initial. If you don't do this, you will negatively affect your self-esteem.

Construction Bump

After reaching an agreement on price, some parties can't help trying for a last bump in the price. This happens frequently when you have negotiated for construction. When they present the written contract, they add on several percentage points because they didn't figure on _____, or the price of $_____ just increased and they are not charging you for the whole increase. They don't think it would be fair, so they are picking up half the increase themselves. Such an increase is planned to be low enough so you don't go elsewhere.

Consider instead taking the position, "A deal is a deal. If prices dropped, I wouldn't expect a reduction in price because $_____ is what I agreed to pay." If you hold firm, the contractor will reluctantly agree to give up what would otherwise have been a bonus.

The Nonexistent Competition

Sellers will raise phantom buyers to make you feel you have competition. If you feel you have competition, your aspirations will be lowered. Buyers often do the same thing, claiming interest in a competitive property. While in most instances the competition is nonexistent, you should realize you might truly be in a competitive position. What risks are you willing to take?

If a buyer or seller is feigning competition, he or she is probably highly motivated. If you can live without the deal, you will be ahead if you consider a claim of competition as simply a negotiating tactic and treat the claim as an affirmation of your power position.

Some sellers are very subtle. They don't tell you that there is a competitor, but they leave unmistakable clues and make slips of the tongue. A secretary might state, "Oh! Are you here about the building on Clark Street?" "You must be Mr. Ogle. I'm so sorry, I had you confused. My appointment book is turned to the wrong page. Mr. Ogle is the other buyer; he won't be in until tomorrow." This apparent slip makes you realize there is another buyer, and the seller never indicated negotiating with anyone else. You will have to reevaluate your position. If you do, you will be doing exactly what your adversary had planned.

A Person You Hate

If you have a strong dislike for a particular firm, this can be used against you if your adversary knows of the animosity. Your adversary could claim the other person is interested in buying the property or has a property he or she wishes to sell your adversary, who will be meeting with your enemy the next day if you're unable to reach agreement. Your opponent will also probably ask you about your enemy. The degree of animosity you show determines how much power you give your adversary. If you are determined that your enemy isn't going to get this deal, chances are you will have succumbed to a very clever bluff. If you follow many other pigeons before you, you will overpay or sell for less, not in your own best interest but to keep an enemy from the deal.

Double Teaming

Japanese purchasers used a double-team approach in purchasing a large California property. The Japanese wanted to party late into the evening, and the American team obliged. Negotiations started early the next morning and continued into the evening. By then, everything but the final price had been covered. About 8 p.m., two Japanese whom the Americans had never met before entered the negotiations. These were the fresh troops who concluded the negotiations with weary adversaries.

If the other side seems intent on tiring you out or if it looks as if there will be a marathon session, consider having informed negotiators on ice, ready to be brought in fresh if you are double-teamed. The way to meet the double-team approach is with your own second team.

Good Guy–Bad Guy

A variation of the good cop–bad cop technique occurs when two persons on the same side disagree, one seemingly undermining the other. The tough person doesn't want to give an inch, while the good guy suggests reevaluation of the position. After a long period of intransigence, the bad guy gets an important call. He tells the good guy to continue but not to give away the store. Their adversary feels the time is ripe for an agreement, and a few concessions will lead to a quick agreement. The third party is very happy and the good guy and bad guy have things according to their plan. Know when this technique is being used against you and realize the concessions the good guy offers are not necessarily all that are possible. The tendency is to feel so relieved that the son of a gun is gone, you let your guard down and your emotions rule. Keep in mind that this really nice guy is a shrewd negotiator and you have just sat through a one-act play put on for your benefit.

The Reluctant Supervisor

This unethical tactic involves a supervisor or associate of the negotiator who comes into the negotiation room. The negotiator introduces the party and then gives a summary of what has been agreed to and what the present positions of the parties are. The supervisor gets distraught and indicates he or she can't approve such an agreement. The negotiator then argues with the supervisor, setting forth the argument of the opposing party. The whole purpose of this charade is to lower the expectations of the other side. The supervisor finally gives in to what the negotiator has given so far. The supervisor leaves. The other party, who was primarily an observer to the battle, probably has vastly lowered expectations, and a quick conclusion, with few significant concessions given to him or her, is likely.

The Intentional Error

An adversary might prepare his or her offer out loud while writing down figures. For example, the party might start with the sale of another property and then add dollars to the value because of special advantages your property has over the other property. The addition will all be in $5,000 or $10,000 increments to allow you to figure the total as they are included The adversary will then add the figures, putting down a price $10,000 more than the addition indicates. Your adversary will hand you the figures and then say, "Let's write the deal up now for [the total dollar amount]." He or she might even start writing up the contract. The math error in your favor is very obvious. What do you do? Many people will sign the contract, thinking of the additional $10,000 they are getting, oblivious to the fact that the price is still inadequate. They have been victims of their own greed, again hoisted on their own petard.

If the offer had not been accepted, the buyer would have discovered his error and lowered the offering price by $10,000. This technique can be used by sellers as well, setting the price $10,000 too low.

Assume your price is both fair and firm. A variation of the intentional error is possible when the buyer states, "I'll give you your full price of $249,000 and the $50,000 down payment you requested, but I want a more realistic interest rate on the $199,000 financing." The offeror will begin writing up the offer at $249,000. You're a little surprised, as you were only asking $239,000. The offer calls for nine percent interest, not the 11 percent stated. Unless you pulled out a financial calculator or an amortization schedule, you are unlikely to realize that carrying a $199,000 loan at nine percent interest will mean $182.39 per month less than a $189,000 loan at 11 percent (based on a 35-year amortization). The net effect to you would be the same as if you had agreed to accept less than $221,000 with the 11 percent financing. Your firm price will have been reduced with a clever error.

Leaving Their Notes

A deceitful tactic used by some negotiators is based on the curiosity and ethical lapses of their opponents. There are a number of variations to this tactic. In one, negotiators leave their material in the room when they take a break or caucus elsewhere. A note pad will be turned upside down so it is obvious you are not intended to see it. You will, however, be given the opportunity to check it. It will reveal a position they are striving for and a maximum (if buying) or minimum (if selling). Of course, the maximum is not the true maximum, and the minimum is not the true minimum. The purpose is to make you think you have an advantage that you can press. When you think you have won, your opponents will have won by their ploy.

Variations of this false data include crumpling papers and throwing them in the wastebasket. A similar variation is to write a position carefully so anyone with any upside down reading skill, which many of us have developed, can read and thus be misled.

Confidential data that is practically handed to you is seldom confidential and unlikely to be accurate.

Writing Notes

Be careful when you write notes or positions down. You could be up against the world's best upside down reader.

If you have notes on the table and the other party complains about the light, watch out if he or she puts on sunglasses—especially, the kind that are mirrored so you can't see the person's eyes. These glasses allow the reader to stare at your notes without your realizing it.

The Nonexistent Partner

Some unscrupulous buyers and sellers will claim they have a partner and tell you that, while there is no problem (as the partner has agreed to go along with what ever they want to do), any agreement will be subject to the partner's approval. After you think you have a deal, the other party states that the partner just won't go for it. They want (as sellers) just a little more or will pay just a little less (as buyers). The difference is generally about two to three percent—enough to make you angry, but probably not enough to make you walk away from the deal.

If the party who mentions a partner is the seller, you as a buyer should request a property profile from a title insurance company. This will reveal if there is in fact a partner. If there is no partner, hold fast. Even if there is a partner, hold fast. It is a negotiation ploy for one last bite of the apple. If you hold firm, it is unlikely the other party will throw away the deal.

A variation used by some parties is to call the nonexistent partner long distance after final approval. Of course, the party you are negotiating with seems like the good guy on the phone, arguing your point of view; but the nonexistent partner won't budge and demands just a little better deal for his or her side.

Whenever a seller attempts to up the price or a buyer attempts to lower it after negotiations are completed, fight fire with fire. By taking a position that you made an error in calculations and must lower your offering price or raise your asking price, you will upset your opponent's plans. Your change in price should be greater than the change demanded by your adversary. You will have set the stage for a final agreement as originally negotiated or, depending on your skill, an even better deal for you to compensate for your time. While we normally can't condone deceit, in a situation such as this we do not view such action as being unethical.

When there is an actual partner, unethical negotiators often do not reveal the partner until negotiations are completed. The party then admits to having a partner but assumes there will be no problem. The partner will want to meet with you and, when he or she does, to use your agreed price as the starting point for new negotiations. Both partners are simply after concessions. Be prepared to use the tactic previously described to counter this type of deception.

Walk-Through

Buyers' offers are usually conditioned upon electrical, mechanical and plumbing systems and appliances being in good working order, and provide for an inspection prior to closing. The "good-old-boy" buyer might turn into the worst nitpicker at the walk-through. What this type of buyer wants is not for additional work to be done, but a last-minute price reduction. The buyer expects something from his or her histrionics so if there is anything you intended to leave which was not specified in the agreement, be prepared to use it as a negotiation chip. These buyers want something, even if it is minor.

Impound Account Thief

An impound account is an escrow account kept by the lender for taxes and insurance. The account is owned by the borrower. Upon sale, the borrower (seller) is entitled to be compensated for the impound account, and taxes and insurance are prorated to date of closing.

Some buyers are using a neat little scam for loan assumptions; their offers state, "Buyer to take over seller's impound account at no cost to buyer and without any proration whatsoever. Taxes and insurance shall, however, be prorated as of date of closing." While this clause appears to be in the buyer's best interest, it is sheer illusion. The buyer is taking over, at no cost, an account that could contain several thousand dollars.

Be on guard against standard forms that don't appear standard and clauses you don't fully understand. See an attorney.

Half-Finished and Renegotiate

A tactic once prevalent among swimming pool contractors, which has also been used by others, is to start work, make a mess and demand a new price. They generally threaten bankruptcy if you don't agree to a higher price, telling you that if they do go into bankruptcy it will tie up the job for years. If you give in to the extortion, they throw in something extra, so that they have given consideration for your agreement to increase the contract price.

If this scam is used against you, contact local building inspectors and get the names of owners for whom they have done other jobs. If checking reveals they have used this tactic before, contact your district attorney.

Subordination

Subordination means to be secondary. A mortgage to be subordinated will take a secondary position to a later recorded mortgage. Whenever an offer includes the word "subordinate," immediately go to a real estate attorney, as chances are someone is trying to take advantage of you.

Because of some seminars on how to buy without cash, there have been a rash of subordination problems around the country. What often happens is the buyer looks for a seller who owns the property free and clear or who has small loans against it. A typical offer would be:

> *"I will give you $200,000 for your home. I will give you $50,000 cash and the $150,000 balance secured by a subordinate mortgage.*

> *"If you accept, I could get a first mortgage for $100,000 (because you have agreed to carry a subordinate mortgage). I would then have the $50,000 to pay you and $50,000 walking-away money in my pocket. I am a cash-out buyer. What would normally happen is that I wouldn't make payments on any of the mortgages and, to stop foreclosure on the first mortgage, you will have to make the payments. You will end up with your house back and a $100,000 lien against it, and I'll end up $50,000 richer."*

Any purchase agreement where the buyer will gain cash should be avoided. He or she has both hands in your pockets.

The Delayed Cash Payout

In Orange County, California, hundreds of homes were purchased by buyers who defrauded the sellers with a unique sales approach. The buyers were looking for homes being sold which had assumable loans. They would usually tell owners they had sold their homes, but the sale was not to close for 90 days. They would offer the seller full price for the property, with an immediate closing and the seller paying all closing costs. The offer provided for the purchaser to assume the existing loan and to cover the balance of the purchase price with a second mortgage that would have no payments but would be paid in full in 90 days. For sellers, these offers looked fantastic and were readily accepted.

The buyers immediately rented the property, often for more than $1,000 a month. They made no payments on the first mortgage. They delayed foreclosure by the lender by claiming fund transfer problems, etc. When the foreclosure process *was* started, it took at least four months. The buyers in the mean time were collecting rents from dozens of properties. The sellers were forced to make the buyers' payments in order to save their equities, and they foreclosed on the second mortgages, which of course were unpaid. Because deficiency judgments are not possible in California for purchase-money loans, the buyers walked away with the rents for periods of time in some cases exceeding one year, with no cash outlay.

This tactic is now a criminal offense in California; and, if intent can be shown, it is fraud elsewhere. However, do not rely on the law after you are defrauded. Be aware of the too-good-to-be-true deal where the buyer enters into possession without cash.

The Savior

Owners who are in danger of losing their property to foreclosure are usually contacted by a number of buyers with schemes they have learned in foreclosure seminars.

One of the tactics used is the savior approach. The person at your door, who might be wearing a clerical collar, will introduce himself and tell you he knows about your foreclosure problem and wants to help. He might tell you how a stranger helped him in a similar difficulty, upon his promise to help another, and he wants to fulfill this obligation. Chances are he has already obtained a property profile and knows what liens are against the house. He will have determined your equity, based on his estimate of value and the amount of your default.

The savior will offer to stop the foreclosure by getting you current on the loan. As security, you will deed the savior your house, but you will have the option of buying it back for exactly what the savior advanced, without any interest, as the savior doesn't believe interest is Christian. You must agree to make rent payments to the savior for the amount of the loan payment.

The agreement seems so reasonable and the answer to your prayers. It is just like in the movies, where the stranger comes along and solves all of the problems by writing the big check. This savior, however, is no movie hero. The kicker is that the option is lost if any payment is more than 10 days late. Since you couldn't make your payments before, chances are you will be late again and you'll have given up a sizable home equity for the advance made to the lender to stop foreclosure. You should now expect an eviction notice almost immediately. Because of abuses of this type, tactics like the one described are a violation of criminal statutes in at least one state.

If you are in foreclosure and you receive a really great offer from someone trying to help you, run, don't walk, to an attorney.

Lis Pendens

A *lis pendens* is a notice of a pending lawsuit. A purchaser who is litigious could find a reason to bring suit over the purchase contract and, by filing a *lis pendens,* could effectively prohibit you from conveying the property to anyone else. If you needed to sell, the *lis pendens* would have the effect of legal blackmail, forcing you to reach an agreement with the buyer that could be very one-sided, based on the buyer's newly found bargaining power.

You can probably protect yourself against a *lis pendens* by having your purchase agreement state, "In the event of seller default the purchaser's sole remedy will be monetary damages, and the purchaser waives any and all right to specific performance."

Because of differing state laws, you should see an attorney about drafting such a provision.

Gazumping

In England, some estate agents practice a tactic called "gazumping," using the first offer to get a higher offer and then going back and forth between buyer and seller in an auction technique. The danger to the buyer is that he or she wants to win over a competitor as much as, or more than, to buy, which often means too high a price.

Reduce Your Offer

If there has been a break of a few days in negotiations, a technique of questionable ethics is to open with an offer less than the offer previously left on the table. For example, if a buyer had offered $400,000 from a previous $385,000, he would go back to the $385,000 offer. The adversary would immediately point out that the buyer had offered $400,000 before. The buyer would act surprised, and look through his notes, and then state,

> *"I don't think that's possible, but if you say I did, I must have, so I'll have to honor my offer. All right, I'll give you an opportunity to accept that offer. Do we have an agreement at $400,000?"*

The Final Zinger

After an agreement has been reached, beware of the final zinger. It's an attempt for a major concession.

> *"I believe I mentioned earlier there will be no payments or interest on the second mortgage for one year."*

Of course, this wasn't previously mentioned. It's an attempt for another bite of the apple, for another chance at your pocketbook. A walk-away technique will normally bring the adversary around to the initial agreement.

The nibbler is a timid zinger. The nibbler wants something minor after the deal has been made. For example, in the purchase of a new car the nibbler will insist on a full tank of gas. In real estate it may be, "You will have to pay for the title insurance." You can either accede to a final extortion of several hundred dollars and leave the nibbler happy, or refuse with great conviction. The nibbler will generally drop his or her demands.

9. The Agreement

A number of the previous chapters covered techniques that lead to closing. This chapter, besides including several general closing tactics, contains suggestions for drafting the agreement, getting it signed, and handling details after signing.

Hold Out Your Hand

The handshake is one of the oldest and easiest methods to close a deal. After you have made what you believe will be your last offer hold out your hand and say, "Do we have a deal?" An extended hand is almost automatically met with a handshake. You have a deal, so write it up.

I Think

A seller can lead to a closing quickly with, "I think $_____ is a fair price. What do you think?" If the other side agrees, you have a deal. If not, ask, "What do you consider a fair price?" This gives you an offer to be negotiated upward.

Let's Get It Over With

This straightforward approach is very effective when you have negotiated for some time and are still a ways apart on price:

> *"Darn, let's get this over with. I know you want to sell, and you know I am willing to buy. You want the best price for you, and I want the best price for me. Let's call it $_____ and reach an agreement right now."*

The Verbal Offer

Real estate agreements must be in writing to be enforceable.

When you have received a verbal offer you are willing to accept, you should say, "Let's see what the offer looks like in writing." Start writing up the offer, and work with your adversary to make certain the document correctly and fully reflects what has been offered. Now hand the offer and a pen to the person making the offer, marking the place for signature. Your adversary must sign or lose credibility. You can then sign and form a binding agreement.

Never allow any part of the understanding to be just an understanding. Make certain it is part of the written agreement, over the signatures.

"By the Way"

After an agreement has apparently been reached, a party might bring up a point as an apparent afterthought. Often it is preceded with "By the way" or "I don't want to forget." It could be "The price does not include. . . ." Whatever it is, it's not likely to be a minor point, although the other side may treat it as such, hoping you're now happy with the basic deal so you're willing to give in on other points.

The Written Offer

You can have an offer form completed except for price and/or financing before your meeting with the owners. After exploratory questioning, you then simply take out your offer, fill in the price and/or other needed items, sign it, and hand the offer and a pen to the owners. It is an extremely effective closing. When they have paper and pen in hand, they have been conditioned to signing.

Write It Up

Your opponent has not agreed to your position but has made the last concession. An excellent technique for closing is to start writing up the agreement, not saying anything, but making a concession in the written offer. When you are finished, hand the signed offer form with a pen to your adversary and state, "Damn, you're the toughest negotiator I've ever worked with!"

You have complimented your opponent, and presented him or her with a written offer reflecting a concession. You have made acceptance very easy for your adversary. Don't say anything. Let your adversary read the offer. If after reading it your adversary puts it down or otherwise hesitates, a simple "Right now you're just a signature away from owning (or selling) _____," can be extremely effective.

Don't Give the Seller Too Much Time

If you give a seller too long a time to accept, he or she might use your offer to shop for competing offers. If agents other than those involved learn of an offer, they could go to prospective buyers and use your offer to elicit higher offers. The net effect will be that, for a few dollars more, someone else will have taken advantage of your efforts.

Agents should keep their open offers confidential and not reveal them to anyone, even within their own offices. Even if their associates don't use the information, there is the danger they will tell someone else who will.

Give parties only a short period to accept written offers. Too much time and they will seek advice of friends and relatives. Many deals have been lost by advice from well-intentioned people who were not qualified to give professional real estate opinions. Worse yet are the cases where people sought advice from others and the persons consulted have met the offer—taking advantage of all the work of another.

If your adversary is pushing you for an immediate acceptance of a written agreement, be on guard. Even if the offer appears favorable, make certain you fully understand all terms. At the very least, consult with your attorney by phone before signing.

Quick Acceptance

When you accept the other party's position too quickly, that party will feel he/she didn't get a good enough deal.

When you get the offer you want to accept, at least make a move to negotiate. You could use:

> *"Is this the best you can do for me?"*

> *"Damn, you are a little over what we wanted to pay (or sell for), but I guess I'll have to live with it. You're tough to deal with. Let's write it up."*

This reinforces the ego of your opposition, reducing the chance of increased demands and/or nonperformance.

You Be the One To Hesitate

When an agreement has been made, a technique to make certain it will be signed is to draft the document, asking the other party if he or she couldn't reduce the price or raise the offer, which will likely be refused. While staring at the offer, take pen in hand and appear ready to sign; then put it down. Finally, take the pen and slowly sign the agreement.

Because of your great hesitancy, your adversary will feel you're not happy with the agreement and will reinforce his or her perception of being a winner. You have materially reduced the likelihood that your adversary will balk at signing.

The best closing is one in which your adversary thinks he or she is the one convincing you to sign.

Teetering

When you indicate difficulty in deciding, it invites a final push or concession. Your indecision will likely give you something extra you didn't even have to ask for.

Teetering has been developed by some into an art form. They never give a position but can't make up their minds. The proposal gets better and better as sweeteners are added.

Poker Face

Never appear elated at an offer or concession. Keep a straight face. Even if you don't want to risk a counteroffer, ask questions. Ask for a little more time. Too quick a decision and the opponents may reconsider their offer.

Overkill

When you see an agreement, go for it. Going for the last drop of blood all too often results in an agreement not closed or no agreement at all.

When you have power, use it carefully so the other party does not resent you. You must be sensitive to his or her needs.

Letting your adversaries squeeze a small final concession from you they will make them feel like winners. They'll know they got the best deal possible.

Subject to My Husband's Approval

Often one spouse will negotiate and arrive at a price subject to the approval of the other spouse, who is unavailable. When you negotiate in these circumstances, save a minor concession.

The problem is that the other spouse often does not hold his or her spouse's negotiation ability in the highest regard and will try to use the agreed-upon price as a new asking price for negotiation. The spouse will try to convey that, since he/she must approve, he/she is in a position of power. Don't believe it. He or she has little power, because failure to approve will result in a confrontation with the other spouse. Let him or her know what a tough negotiator the spouse was; then take a hard-line approach on attempts to lower the price. Say that you have already reduced it too far. To make him or her happy that he or she got something for the additional effort, you can now give up the concession you saved initially.

Control the Drafting

If an agreement is to be drafted rather than put on a standard form, keep accurate notes and, if possible, control the drafting. For protection, have it either drafted or approved by your attorney prior to signing. Keep in mind that ambiguities are resolved against the party drafting the instrument. This points out the need for legal review.

To avoid fading memories, have all parties sign a brief memo in outline form, setting forth the points of agreement.

You don't want the agreement to scare the other party. Try for language that is clear. Avoid legal terms whenever possible. Use short sentences and headings that describe what the paragraph contains. Consider a checklist so that nothing will be left out. Make certain all agreements are part of the writing. An oral understanding isn't worth the paper it isn't written on.

If your adversary drafts the agreement, review it carefully. If items were left unresolved, parties drafting the agreement commonly take their own position as to those items.

A Little Too Greedy

A casino in Atlantic City is built around a rooming house. In California, a house is wedged into the rear of a shopping center parking lot. In Milwaukee, a small house and lot are dwarfed by two large apartment towers. In all three instances, the owners held out for just a little more, and the little more was just a little too much. The parties in these instances believed they were negotiating from positions of power, and they were; but power is not absolute. At some point their adversaries said, "Enough" and made plans without them. If you know the other party needs your property, you should evaluate the economic consequences of uses that don't include your property. If you are wrong, you could not only lose a sale but have little economic value left for your property.

The Insecure Agent

The real estate agent who is insecure is often an unknowing ally of the purchaser. Agents sometimes want the deal so badly they will push acceptance of offers not really in the best interests of the seller. While unethical, such conduct nevertheless is all too frequently a reality. As a seller, you should realize your agent might have a personal conflict when his or her interests are not necessarily identical with yours.

Redline the Agreement

When presenting a contract you have drafted for signature, consider having a copy with the specific areas of original disagreement underlined in red or highlighted. It makes it easy for your adversary to see you have accurately set forth what was agreed upon.

Some parties use redlining in an unethical manner, which is why you should read the entire agreement carefully before signing. They will be accurate in what they have redlined but will sneak in clauses favorable to them which were not agreed on and which are not highlighted, hoping you won't catch the error.

The Best Negotiations

The best negotiation is one in which your adversary is pleased with the agreement. If he or she is displeased, the party may not honor the agreement, using any unexpected problem as a reason to void your contract.

You can lessen this possibility by giving a little something extra to your adversary after agreement has been reached. Further reinforcement would be to tell them they stretched you to your limit. You were not prepared to pay more than $_____ or sell for less than $_____. An adversary who feels you didn't get your expectations will regard himself or herself as a winner, unlikely to try to breach the agreement.

One professional negotiator likes to carry different pieces of paper in various pockets. He tells his adversary after negotiation, "You know, you've put me in the position of having to justify what I agree to. My boss told me to walk away if I couldn't get it for $325,000, and I have agreed to pay considerably more. I have his note right here." He then reaches into a pocket and hands over a well-worn, folded piece of paper. The seller opens the paper and written on it is "Maximum Price $325,000." It would be extremely embarrassing if he gave the wrong slip quoting a price higher than agreed to, but he apparently has a system that works.

Never Tell

Several years ago, the author taught a graduate course in negotiation technique. An exercise that continued over eight weeks was a mock negotiation, with each side given separate sets of facts, what they believed their adversaries' positions were and why. Weekly information was given to each team. After negotiations were completed, both sides considered themselves winners. The teams were then given their opponents' positions and facts at their disposal. The result was predictable—anger at the other team for deception—and both teams now regarded themselves as losers because they realized they could have gotten more or paid less. They learned that coups on issues as they were resolved were not coups at all but phantom issues raised as negotiation chips. Both sides were angry. If they could, they would want to get out of their agreement.

The lesson learned is never reveal your true position after negotiating is over. Don't rub your adversary's face in the fact that you're ecstatic with your deal and would have paid more or sold for less. On the contrary, reinforce the view that he or she got the best of you.

If you want to rejoice, wait until you're alone. Never tell others how you bettered your opponent, as it will likely get back to him.

Don't worry how the other side does, or perceives how they did. Some foolish negotiators will tell you they would have paid much more or sold for much less after negotiations are concluded. They are doing this for their own egos, and what they say is seldom true. Consider only what you have accomplished for yourself. If you have come out satisfactorily, based on your criteria, you are a winner.

Lis Pendens

If the seller tries to get out of your agreement by entering into a sale agreement with another party or by placing the property on the market, consult an attorney about a *lis pendens* action, which serves to notify all parties of your asserted right to the property. A *lis pendens* is a privileged action; and any action by the owner as to malicious prosecution, slander of title or abuse of process must generally wait until your claim is adjudicated.

A *lis pendens* action should not be started lightly, as you could subject yourself to damage if your action is improper; but for a just claim it will usually result in the seller honoring his or her agreement.

They Don't Leave It

If the sellers take personal property or fixtures they had agreed to leave, don't hesitate to contact them and demand the return. The longer you wait, the less the chance they will voluntarily return the property.

If they indicate they will not return the property, consider an action in small claims court. Costs are usually minimal, and, depending on the state, claims for amounts up to several thousand dollars can be handled. Have the notice served by a sheriff or a marshall, if possible. Serving the notice will often result in the return of the property prior to the court date.

Index

189

Lies and mistakes, 54, 168–69
Limited partnerships, 127–28
Liquidated damages, 155
Lis pendens, 175, 187
Litigious people, 9–10, 175
Loan assumption, 106, 107, 111–12, 122–23, 172, 173–74
Loan negotiations, 118–20
"Low-balling," 162–63
Low offers, 14–15, 162–64
Lunchtime negotiations, 158

M
MAI (Member of the Appraisal Institute), 7, 162
Manager's apartment, 157–58
Mediation, 148
Momentum, breaking, 70–71
Moratorium on payments and interest, 107–08, 122
Motivations and needs, 8, 41–42

N
Naming the building, 128–29
Negative loan amortization, 107
Negotiating
    financing, 105–20
    issues other than price and financing, 121–32
    physical aspects of, 27–32, 76, 138–39
    price, 81–104, 122; see also Impasse
Negotiation
    dangers of, 153–77
    phone, 5
    physical aspects of, 27–32, 76, 138–39
    planning, 1–25
    points, 20
    risks of, 4
    successful, 186
    tactics, 33–79; see also other chapter headings
    taking charge, 34
Negotiator, qualities of a good, 1–2
Neighbors, checking with, 11
Neutral ground, 28

New building allowance, 155
Nonexistent competition, 166
Nonexistent partners, 170–71

O
Obstacles, anticipating, 15–17; see also Impasse
Occupancy prior to closing, 158
Offsetting price, 122
One-price seller, 87
Open analysis, 140
Open issue, 123
Opening and closing statements, 21
"Other" properties, 57–58

P
Paper payments, 110, 162
Participative solutions, 141
Payment penalties, 114
Personal attacks, 36–38
Personal property, 127, 188
Personal rapport, 39–40
Personality conflicts, 35–36, 134, 166–67
Phone negotiations, 5
Physical aspects of negotiation, 27–32, 76, 138–39
Physical tactics, 44–47
Planning, 1–25, 86–87
Points, 94, 114–15
Power, definition, 17
Power dressing, 31–32
Predictable people, 14–15
Prepayment penalties, 114
Presentations, preparing, 18
Price negotiation, 81–104, 154, 165
Price reduction in lieu of work, 154
Prioritizing, 18
Problem solving, 55–56; see also Impasse; Negotiation, dangers of
Promises, 35
Property profiles, 14
Purchase offers, requests for, 42
Purchase price, original, 13

Q–R
Questioning during negotiations, 47, 49, 59